SOME PEOPLE ARE

STUPID,

BUT NOT YOU!

Stories about humility,
Perseverance, and Giving Back

JAMES A. FABER

Dedication

For Suzanne and the Children

Table of Contents

Introduction

"Whenever you are to do a thing, though it can be never known but to yourself, ask yourself how you would act were all the world looking at you, and act accordingly."

Thomas Jefferson

We all have a story to tell and something each of us can learn from them. The purpose of this book is to share some "observations and life lessons" based on over three decades of service and counting. I share stories and experiences having grown up in poverty, serving in the Air Force as a Lt. Colonel, Non-profit CEO, Entrepreneur, President of two disability rights organizations and most importantly, a husband and father. In every case I have always tried to put others ahead of myself and have made my share of mistakes along the way. I did not write this book to boast about my accomplishments or to set the record straight, but rather to share some things I have learned which I hope at least one reader finds useful

The stories in this book are all based on actual events across several different careers and experiences. The writing of this book has been a "work in progress" for a few years and I have learned a lot about vulnerability in sharing these stories. In every case I have tried to present the story as it actually occurred and to share the lesson I learned from it. This book is my attempt to highlight the important things we all experience and how we can learn from them and share with others. We are all better together.

We learn and grow as a community, nation, and world when we talk, listen, and agree or disagree in a civil manner all aimed at the "Pursuit of a more perfect Union." Each story ends with the relevant lesson learned from my perspective and I hope readers will take away their own lessons from the stories. In every case I have tried to convey the stories as a way for all of us to listen and learn from each other. I believe we are all lifelong learners and should try to learn something new every day. If one reader finds inspiration, motivation, laughter, or insight from one of these stories then for that, I will be eternally grateful!

Enjoy and feel free to send me your feedback.
Jim
www.jimfaber.com

Chapter 1
Growing Up Average

I was born in Somerville, MA, just outside of Boston, in a low-income neighborhood. As a kid growing up, I did not realize or understand that we were low-income and I was just one of the neighborhood kids. My brother and I would play in the courtyard between the long red brick buildings where all the tenants hung their laundry to dry. I recall running through the hanging laundry and pretending we were "flying" through some bizarre multi-colored cloud layer.

"Albie," I would call to my brother, "I am a bird soaring through the clouds."

"Yeah," Albie exclaimed, while twirling his arms and running through the rows of laundry, "I am an airplane flying through the mountains!"

In the background of our "flying adventures," there was the ever-present aroma of the hot asphalt, clean laundry, and strange "musky" smell that emanated from the open apartment windows. The combination of these aromas created a sharp, sweet, and moldy smell that assaulted the senses, but never bothered us since this was the smell of home.

My old neighborhood was not known as being a desirable place to live and even today has a high crime rate, but all I knew growing up was that I wanted to stay out of trouble and eventually leave the neighborhood. Staying out of trouble was harder than one might realize and I often found myself in trouble for one thing or another, or on the fringes of it, since the circle of friends I ran with were always finding ways to get us into trouble or arrested. I was growing up to be a good juvenile delinquent, and it is not that my parents were bad people, or uncaring, but in our situation, parents tend to focus more on finding money to pay the rent than they do on the daily activities of their children. In addition, the divorce rate is high among these types of families and mine was no exception, as my parents divorced when I was about nine years old. This is not a sad story or an excuse; rather, it is a typical American story that repeats itself daily in our country. The difference is what you make of a negative environment.

The "culture of poverty" has been well documented and studied for a number of years and often people living in poverty tend to have extreme feelings of helplessness, a strong dependency on others in the same circumstance, and a feeling of marginality and powerlessness. I would try to engage in conversations with my parents and hear many of the same refrains as if the tape was stuck on repeat.

"Mom," I would ask, "why do we live here in this place if you hate it so much?"

"Well," she would reply, "the system is broken and does not afford many opportunities to people in our situation."

"If the system is broken, Mom," I blurted out, "then why don't we try to change it or why can't we figure out a way to do better under the flawed system?"

"Jimmy," she replied, "you are young and do not understand how hard it is when every time you start to make headway, someone throws out another roadblock."

It just seemed useless to have these conversations since both my parents would always "blame" some external factor for our situation rather than acknowledging their own bad decisions and how those contributed to the downward spiral. Of course, there is also a systemic component to the issue of poverty which perpetuates itself, but there are also choices and decisions that require hard work and persistence to help reverse the "cycle of poverty." The constant belief that we had no say in how things were and the feeling that "this is as good as it gets and ever will be" was depressing at times. I refused to accept that and committed myself to figuring out how to make things better for myself and maybe those around me as long as they did not try to pull me backwards. This determination was perhaps a blessing I did not fully understand or appreciate in the moment, but it led me to making some very tough and uncomfortable decisions.

There are many adults with a similar story and many more that never overcame their upbringing due to the overwhelming odds against them. Poverty is like a terrible equalizer in what might be an unequal system according to some pundits, but the fact remains it is like an anchor weighing you down. It is very challenging for all persons who come from a low-income background to break the cycle of poverty and all journeys out of low-income are not equal, as some have it much harder than others. Growing up average is how a lot of Americans are raised and it takes a spark, a mentor, hero, internal drive, divine intervention, or some other inspiration to realize that with hard work you can be anything you want to be. The low-income culture is one of mutual dependence and it is hard to break away from it. This is home and as flawed as it may be, these are the people who raised you, love you, and would do most anything for you. The cycle of poverty is like "comfort food" and when you live there with everyone you have grown up with, it is like a very comfortable blanket on a cold winter's day when you do not want to get out of bed. Eventually there is a tug, a voice, or inspired intervention that says, "You need to get up and brave the cold. Eventually you will be warm again, but for now you need to throw off the comfortable blanket and get on with it."

How hard is that when others you know and love refuse to "get out of bed" despite your pleas and hopes that we can do better?

I was constantly being told that I would never amount to anything and when I did try to better myself, the adults around me would say, "Who do you think you are? Do you think you are better than us?"

The short answer was always, "No, I do not think I am any better than anyone else."

I just knew that I did not want the same type of life that was surrounding me, so I always stayed focused on my dreams, as distant as they seemed. I realized at an early age that hard work would be my only salvation and that there would be no free handouts or access to opportunities while trying to "break the cycle" of poverty and averageness.

There were kids I knew growing up that came from a much better situation and had supportive parents that knew the value of hard work and a good education. I must admit that I was jealous that these kids had access to opportunities that I did not and often times they did not appreciate it. I am not saying that these kids had it easier than I did to be successful. What I am saying is that the opportunities were a bit more accessible for these kids than a poor white trash Irish kid having to create my own opportunities. When I got invited onto the dance floor, I took it very seriously and worked harder than most others since I knew I might not get another chance. I watched in awe as several of my "better off" friends were presented with these opportunities, only to squander them and fall back on their family support system. These kids could not understand how a kid from the "Somerville projects" was beating them in peer-to-peer competition when I got the chance to get on the dance floor. They were told their whole lives how extraordinary they were, how successful they would be, and what high expectations their parents had. Something was missing and they could not see what it was.

Growing up average would have served these kids much better. In today's society, I see it all the time among my peers in the upper middle class stratum. Parents that I know, and others I see in my children's school district, are constantly telling their children how special and unique they are. These children are growing up thinking that just because they are alive and breathe oxygen they are extraordinary human beings destined for greatness. I am not trying to say that parents should not encourage their children or tell them they are special, but this must be tempered with the hard truth that true greatness and success are the results of hard work. Often, failure is a large part of success and children today need to understand that sometimes they will fail or fall short, but that is never an excuse to quit. The number of times I failed or had an obstacle placed in my way only emboldened me to find another path to achieve my goals. Many times I had to take detours when certain opportunities did not present themselves, or I failed at something. I always stayed focused, and although some of the paths were the "long way around," I eventually got there. I fear this is missing today among many of the families I interact with and I am noticing arrogance among many young adults who think they are entitled to greatness or a successful career—you are not.

I have decided to label this phenomenon the "Reality TV/Social Media Syndrome." I am not much of a TV watcher, other than sporting events, but one show I tend to follow is American Idol and, in particular, the audition shows. I really like watching the auditions and seeing some of the incredible talent that tries out for the show and is rejected. Many of these people are told to continue pursuing their dreams and several have come back for second auditions and have made the show. I like seeing young people trying their best, falling down, and then getting up again and working harder—this is the essence of the American Spirit. I was always motivated to get back up every time I fell down and work harder to improve and reach my goals.

During auditions, the show features several young people that have somehow grown up thinking they are entitled to greatness or are blinded by their own passion. The show's producers put some of the less than talented auditions through to the judge round simply to get ratings, but regardless, the complete lack of reality in some of their lives is very worrisome. It is obvious to me that several young people that audition have grown up in a world where everyone in their immediate family told them constantly how great and talented they were. Perhaps the family really believed that their child was the next biggest thing in show business. However, after learning that they were not, they typically fail to alter their opinion. I am always surprised at how the judges can listen to an impossible audition and tell the person they have absolutely no singing talent, but they insist that they do. It gets worse when the cameras follow the person who then consults with their parents and family members who all say the judges have no clue what they are talking about. This is when it gets funny as some choice words and gestures are thrown at the cameras and they exclaim how they will carry on singing. Constructive feedback and critique are a part of life and it is how we grow, mature, and become better versions of ourselves. Perhaps these young people could also have used a little "growing up average" in their lives.

In my personal experience raising four children, I think it is very important that we support, encourage, and assist our children in everything they do, but we also need to "keep it real." There are some parents that might read this and disagree and say they will continue to promote their child as the greatest there is. I am OK with that, but perhaps we can all try a little bit of humility, which could go a long way in creating a better place for all of us to live. Daily I see people who are obviously living lives below the greatness they were promised, but still cling to the idea that they are great, rather than doing the hard work. This leads to people that tend to care only for themselves and their immediate family and are a bit self-centered. Just look at all the reality TV shows and social media platforms that have emerged over the past few decades celebrating the lives of otherwise very ordinary people. Imagine what would happen if we all worked hard for the greatness we seek and actually earned the respect and accolades of others for real life accomplishments? I think we tend to award and praise people for mediocre performance and accomplishments, which perpetuates the "Reality TV/Social Media Syndrome." Let's praise, award, celebrate, and cheer for the real heroes who are making a difference in the lives of others. Let's all try being average for a while.

Some People Are Stupid, but Not YOU, Because:

You know being average and understanding that hard work,
persistence and never giving up leads to true greatness
in every aspect of our lives, which is earned, not entitled.

Chapter 2
Becoming More than Average

When I was eight years old, I attended my first air show at Naval Air Station Quonset Point, Rhode Island, where I experienced the thrill and excitement of high-performance jets for the first time. I was immediately hooked on the notion of flying airplanes someday, as so many young dreamers are. The idea of flying high performance jets seemed as distant as the moon, but definitely within reach. I recall an aerial demonstration by the Navy's Blue Angels flight team that I can still see as vividly today as the when I first saw the demonstration. The Blue Angels were flying F-4s in the early seventies, which at the time was one of the most advanced fighters in the US military inventory. I had seen pictures of F-4s and news footage of them flying in the Vietnam War and now I was able to see them for real.

I watched the military precision of the pre-flight, taxi, takeoff, and aerial demonstration as the pilots put the F-4s through some of the most magnificent maneuvers and formations. At the end of the demonstration, the pilots approached the crowd line and talked to us and signed autographs. These guys were superheroes to me and I was eager to get their autographs but did not have an air show program. One of the pilots approached me and handed me a brochure that had pictures of the team and every pilot signed their name. This Blue Angles brochure became a priceless possession and it would grace my bedroom wall for years.

As I was leaving the air show, I turned to my father. "Dad," I said, "someday I am going to fly high performance jets like the Blue

Angels!"

"Yeah right," my father replied in a very dismissive voice and patted me on the head.

It felt like a kick in the stomach. I was hoping for some encouragement or the standard, "you can do anything you set your mind to."

My father was not supportive and provided no reinforcement or encouragement to pursue my dreams. The reality of the "poverty culture" did not leave a whole lot of room for dreams. I felt suffocated in this environment and a few years later, I decided to leave home and escape the physical and mental abuse at the hands of my father and stepmother. As I left my father's house to live with my mother he yelled, "You will never amount to anything!"

Over a decade later and after a long and "indirect" journey, I would be flying the most advanced jets in the world in the US Air Force.

How does a kid from a low-income background end up attending a prestigious university on a full Air Force flight scholarship, attend flight school, and end up flying one of the most advanced airplanes in the Air Force inventory in the mid-1980s? Laser focus, unwavering determination, hard work, and NEVER losing sight of my dreams!

I could not tolerate any naysayers telling me how I was aiming too high and that I would ultimately be disappointed. I had to take several detours along the way as obstacles blocked my path or a door was closed, but I always found a way around and an alternate route that would eventually lead me to my goal. Like I mentioned earlier, this is not a unique or unusual story and it is one we hear often in many different circumstances. This story needs to be re-told, refreshed, and updated continually to remind everyone that they are only limited by their own self-imposed limitations. It is not easy and I agree that along the way I had some luck, but I would say that the harder I worked, the more luck I seemed to have!

I think I was blessed with a strong stubbornness and sheer determination that anything is possible if you set your mind to it. I was nothing special and after making up my mind that I wanted to fly jets in the US Air Force, my life seemed to have a purpose. I was no scholar and had my struggles in high school that so many young adults do. I had to work harder than most of my classmates to learn the same concepts. I was not blessed with a lot of brains, but I did have street smarts, which taught me how to read people and interact with them to support progress toward my goal. I realized early on that to fit into the middle class and have opportunity, I would have to learn how to act like them and become accepted in their circles. I was a poor Irish kid from Boston. I did not receive any special consideration and concluded that I would have to create my own opportunities. It was not easy to fit in, but I knew this was the first step on my journey towards my goal.

I knew that colleges would not consider the public high school I was attending very favorably, and the education was sub-standard at best. I had to get myself into one of the best private high schools in the area, but did not have any connections, resources, or sponsors to open any doors. My family moved to Rhode Island shortly after I started high school and I sought out the best high schools in the area. I eventually took the entrance exam to the private high school I wanted to attend, and after much studying and hard work, I earned a high enough score to apply for admission. I recall the interview with the Christian Brothers who ran the school and talking about my goals and dreams. The brothers knew that I did not have the resources to attend their school and my first attempt for admission was "tentatively approved," which is a nice way of saying you cannot afford to attend. The Christian Brothers did approve a lower tuition rate for me and a "relaxed" payment plan based on what I could afford at any given time. Tuition assistance and other sources of aid were not too abundant in the late seventies, so I needed to figure out a way to pay tuition. I entered my freshman year at a public school but stayed focused on getting into the private school. I did not give up and persisted through the application process.

I worked full time during the summer months and part time during the school year to save enough for tuition payments. By this time, I had earned the respect of a few bosses and they wrote very strong letters of recommendation highlighting my strong work ethic. As a result, I was accepted in my sophomore year to this private high school.

High school is a difficult environment for every teenager as they are maturing into young men and women, dealing with social awkwardness, acceptance, social trends, appropriate behaviors, and the list goes on, but being different adds to the stress of high school. I was different than the majority of my classmates and besides the normal challenges of high school, I also found myself trying to fit in since I did not come from the same socio-economic class. I quickly learned and began to understand what minority populations must frequently feel like when they are among the majority. I was a "minority subset" of the majority due to my socio-economic status and knew there was much work to be done to fit in. At least I looked like everyone else, so my task would be much easier on the surface of things. Early on I decided to stay focused on the most important thing—my education and life goal to fly Air Force jets someday. I did all the usual things in high school to build my resume (track team, debate team, student council, etc.), and most importantly studied hard to letter in academics. I earned placement on the Dean's List and graduated cum laude with a good enough GPA to be accepted into several prestigious universities.

College was going to be difficult since I had the same resource challenges as I did for high school, and I was also the first person in my family to ever attend college. The adults around me did not understand why I was wasting my time trying to go to college and worked to convince me my high school diploma was sufficient to land a great job.

In the seventies, going to college was more of an exception than a standard practice and successfully completing high school was a bigger deal than it seems to be today. The United States has come a long way since then in promoting the importance of a post-secondary education and has provided billions of dollars to support higher education.

I applied to several colleges and universities and was accepted to several schools "conditionally," pending tuition assistance, grants, and scholarships. I also tried to go to the Air Force Academy, but did not receive a nomination from any of my elected representatives, so I was unable to apply for admission. It became apparent that I would not be able to attend some of the more expensive and prestigious universities due to my limited access to resources, so I developed a Plan B. Staying focused on my goal of flying Air Force jets, I decided to attend a small aviation college in New Hampshire my freshman year to study Aviation Management and earn my pilot's license. The school was very affordable and with the work-study program, tuition assistance, grants, scholarships, and money I had saved, there was enough to cover the first year's tuition. In addition to tuition costs, there were additional fees for the flying aspect of the degree program and I had saved enough money to allow me to take flying lessons the first semester of my freshman year. Things were not going exactly as planned, but I had found a detour that allowed me to attend college and start flying.

The first semester of my freshman year was extraordinary. I was learning so much across multiple disciplines and, most importantly, I was learning about aviation and flying. During my first semester, after weeks of ground school, I had my very first flight. I was nervous since I had never flown before and did not know if aviation would be a good fit for me. I had been so enthralled with the idea of flying for so long that I never thought about the "what if I hate flying" side of things.

Luckily, I learned during my first flight that I absolutely loved flying, and for once in my life, I finally felt I was in control. I was not a natural born flyer, and I doubt anyone really is, but I did enjoy every aspect of being airborne and it motivated me to work very hard at all the basic skills required to be a good pilot. A few weeks after my first flight, and with only eight hours of total flight time, I was signed off to solo and I will never forget that amazing experience. I learned during my solo flight that anything is possible if you work hard enough, and I was one step closer to my dream. I had also joined Air Force ROTC during my freshman year and made it clear from the beginning that I would be competing for a pilot slot. I became a cadet airman basic and set about learning all I could in my aerospace studies classes with the eventual goal of earning an officer's commission and flight slot. Life could not be better and I felt as though I was finally on my way.

After my first semester of freshman year, the reality of limited resources once again reared its head and I was thrown another curve ball. I had managed to pull together enough resources to cover the tuition for my freshman year, but several of these sources would not be available for my sophomore year. It soon became apparent that I would not be returning for my sophomore year and my college education was about to end. I was not certain what to do and I applied for every type of financial aid, grants, and loans you could imagine, but I was still unable to make ends meet. Despite this lack of resources, I felt lucky that I was able to at least have a year of undergraduate study and, most importantly, experience flying. I was determined not to give up and expected that I would simply return home and work like I had done in the past and continue my education anyway I could. My plan was to take night and weekend courses at the local university and continue flying lessons as time and money permitted. In the meantime, I remained committed to my studies, was working hard in Air Force ROTC, and was also considering enlisting to earn education benefits. The path towards my goal was once again detoured and I would have to take the longer way around, which by this point in my life was standard and accepted practice.

Towards the end of my freshman year and faced with the prospect of not returning, I received amazing and unexpected news. The lieutenant colonel commanding my ROTC detachment, known as the Professor of Aerospace Studies (PAS), came into our airmanship class one day looking rather upset about something. The colonel announced that he had received a report that a freshman cadet was out of uniform and that this was completely unacceptable. I sat in my chair thinking about how I had spent so much time ensuring every detail of my uniform was perfect and I did not envy the freshman that was out of compliance.

The colonel then unexpectedly called out, "Cadet Faber, front and center."

My heart jumped out of my chest!! I stood up, came to attention, squared my corners, marched to the front of the class, saluted the colonel, and remained standing at attention. I was shocked and wondered what I had done and why my uniform was not in compliance. My classmates had terrible looks on their faces since drawing the attention of the commanding officer for being out of compliance did not exactly further one's career aspirations.

The colonel looked at me and asked, "Cadet Faber, do you have any idea what is wrong with your uniform?"

I meekly answered, "No sir, I am unaware why my uniform is out of compliance."

This was it; the colonel turned to me and said, "You are out of compliance because you are not wearing a required badge on your uniform."

I was perplexed to say the least, and did not understand what the colonel was talking about since as a cadet airman basic we did not really have many authorized badges beyond our rank and nametag. The colonel then extended his hand towards me and opened it to reveal a set of cadet wings. The only cadets that wore wings were the juniors and seniors that had already taken the oath and received a flight slot.

The colonel then announced, "Based on Cadet Faber's performance to date and test scores, I am pleased to announce that the Air Force had awarded him a full four-year flight scholarship retroactive to the beginning of freshman year!"

I nearly fell over. I had no idea I was even being considered for such an honor. I learned that underclassman were allowed to wear wings only if they were on a full flight scholarship, and at that moment, I was out of uniform. I pinned on those wings as quickly as I could and suddenly my college education was secured.

I ended up leaving the small aviation college in New Hampshire to attend Boston University. The flight scholarship paid for tuition, books, fees and a portion of board, but it would not pay for the flight lessons that were part of the Aviation Management Degree Program. Since I could not afford to fly anymore, I decided it was best to use the scholarship to earn a straight business degree from a more prestigious university. My education was the most important thing, and I was given the chance to attend any university that would accept me. In addition, the flight scholarship I was awarded was not a pilot scholarship, but a navigator scholarship, since that was what the Air Force needed and pilot scholarships were not being offered. Yet another curveball, but I was lucky and very fortunate that I would earn my college education, receive a 2nd Lieutenant's Commission, and still get the chance to fly the most advanced jets in the world.

Some People Are Stupid, but Not YOU, Because:

You understand that the harder we work, the luckier we become, and even when road blocks get in our way, we stay focused on the ultimate goal and find alternate routes.

Chapter 3
Smell the Roses

In 1983, I was in my second year of college on a full Air Force flight scholarship. I counted my blessings daily and was working very hard to do well in all of my classes and Air Force ROTC. I was fortunate to have been promoted ahead of my peers in ROTC, and was selected to command the local chapter of the Arnold Air Society. In addition, I had applied to Boston University (BU) and was accepted to start in the fall and join the BU Air Force cadet wing as a cadet officer. The spring semester was busy trying to ensure I was taking all the right courses required for the AF scholarship and the BU program I had been accepted into. The academic demands were challenging, and coupled with the ongoing demands of the ROTC program, I had very little free time. I was also preparing for my transfer to BU and a required two-week Air Force field training program at the end of the semester. My summer was planned so I could attend field training, work part-time, take two additional math classes required for my scholarship, and start at BU in September 1983. The hard work was paying off and I felt I was finally on my way to achieving my dream; life was good. Then suddenly, life took an unexpected turn.

It was late January 1983, and I had been back at school for a few weeks after the holiday break. Classes were busy as usual, and the semester was off to a good start. One day when I returned to my room, there was a phone message taped to my door. The message read, "Please call home as soon as possible." In the mid-80s we did not have cellphones and the entire dorm shared one central payphone, so taking messages was the only way to reach somebody. It seemed a bit unusual to me since I rarely received phone calls, so I went to the payphone and called home. My older brother, Steven, answered the phone. "Hello," my brother said.

"Steven," I said, "is that you? Why are you answering mom's phone?"

Steven started, "Jimmy, I have terrible news. Susan (my sister) has passed away."

"What?" I exclaimed. "What happened?"

The shock of what my brother had just said hit me like a ton of bricks and I could not believe it. My sister was only twenty-two and a bright, happy person that was always supportive and encouraging of my dreams and goals. Steven then said, "She had a heart attack, which may have been brought on by an overdose of narcotics. You need to come home right away."

"I thought Susan was doing well," I said. "Over Christmas break she was wonderful and full of life!"

"Well," Steven continued, "she did like to experiment once in a while, and we think she overdosed on a combination of heroin and cocaine."

I could not believe it. I knew she had occasionally experimented, but she was not a drug addict and was getting her life together.

My family home was not a great environment, and with an alcoholic mother and an uncle who was a convicted murderer, there were always drugs around. I recall the detectives assigned to my sister's case coming to the house to interview me. The manner of her death was suspicious, so they were conducting an investigation to ensure there had not been any foul play. The detective introduced himself and asked a bunch of standard questions about my sister and her mental health. I said, "She was very happy and had recently completed beauty school and was getting everything together."

"Did she have a drug problem?" the detective asked.

I defensively said, "What does that matter at this point?"

I surprised myself when I said this, and how defensive I had become, since I could not understand how this information would do anything to make the situation better or bring my sister back.

The detective continued, "I am sorry to ask, but it is a standard question."

I replied, "I am not going to say anything about my sister except I love her very much and none of this matters."

I thought the detective might fire back at me, but instead he said, "I understand, but you should know that the coroner is saying the heart attack was caused by an overdose of cocaine and heroin."

"I know," I said. "She made a mistake and paid a huge price."

"OK," the detective said. "That is good enough for us. And this house is already known to us, so we will likely conclude in our report that it was an overdose."

My house was well known to the local police since people were always coming and going. The police typically were called to my house at least once a month for some manner of domestic disturbance and they knew drugs were part of the equation. I explained that this was the reason I was in school and trying to get out of this environment. The detectives were satisfied and encouraged me to continue on my path, but it was too late for my sister. She had not been so lucky.

At my sister's funeral, I was in a complete state of shock and went through the motions of saying goodbye to my sister, whom I loved very much. She was a bright light in my life and had always been proud of what I was trying to do and very supportive. I had lost one of my closest friends and confidants. I was feeling lost. As I said my final goodbye to my sister, I vowed right then that I would re-double my efforts to get out of this environment and make a better life for myself. The strange thing about losing a close loved one so young, besides the tragedy of it, is that a sort of fog descends over your life. I found myself working harder than ever, which no doubt was my coping mechanism. Things did not have the same color as they did before and it was harder to find courage and optimism about the future. During this time, I read an article where the author described this mourning period as a "period of temporary insanity" that lasts for about two years. Only time would tell how long it would be before I would begin to feel normal again.

I returned to school and got on with my classwork. All my school friends were sympathetic, but it all seemed so surreal to me. I was pleased as the semester drew to a close and I was finished with finals. I had planned to leave the campus as soon as possible and only spend a few days at home before I shipped off for my Air Force training. My goal was to spend as little time at home as possible to avoid that environment and the possibility of being caught up in something that might derail my future in the Air Force. I focused on the next thing and headed off to upper state New York for my Air Force field training. It was nice to be in a new environment where nobody knew anything about me or what had happened. In a way, it helped me to not have reminders all the time about my tragic loss and the "How are you doing?" questions.

Air Force field training was going well and we were doing a lot of physical training, marching, and attending classes. The strict discipline and the very busy days really helped me cope, or at least avoid coping, with my sister's death. My class was only two days from graduation. It felt really good to be nearly done and we were busy preparing for the graduation ceremonies. I was in the base chapel attending a final lecture on ethics and responsibility when I got a tap on my shoulder. I turned to see our flight sergeant, who said, "Cadet Faber, the flight commander needs to see you right away."

"Ok," I said and followed him to the commander's office.

My flight commander was an active duty Air Force major and I proceeded to report into his office. Before I could salute and report in, he said, "Cadet Faber, please be at ease and have a seat."

This was very unusual since we had spent the last two weeks marching everywhere and saluting everything that moved! The commander continued, "I have terrible news I must share with you. Your father has passed away."

At first, I did not really hear what he said, and found myself reliving my sister's death that had occurred only five months earlier. This was a second shock to the system, and although he said it was my father, it was actually my stepfather. My real father had abandoned us many years before and this man had married my mother and was a very strong and positive influence on me when I was a teenager. My stepfather was a flawed man, but at the same time, a warm-hearted person who showed me some of the finer sides of life and encouraged me to pursue my dreams. He came into my life when I was a teenager and diverted me from going down the wrong path, which can be very alluring to a teenager growing up in my environment. I was very close to him and really cared deeply for him.

"What happened?" I asked.

My commander said, "I do not have all the details, but I think it was some kind of a stroke."

The major continued, "I also heard you lost your sister just a few months ago. I feel terrible about this news and we are here for whatever you need."

"Of course," he said, "we have started making arrangements to get you home as soon as possible. You have successfully completed all the training requirements, so leaving a day early will in no way impact your graduation from the program."

I really had no words at this point and could not believe my stepfather had passed away at such a young age; he was only in his mid-fifties and in good health. I left field training to attend my second funeral in five months and would learn that my stepfather had a headache and went to see the doctor. He was admitted to the hospital for tests, but before they could figure out what was happening, he had a brain aneurysm and died within a few hours of arriving at the hospital. Yet another tragedy, and I felt the fog around me begin to get heavier.

After my stepfather's funeral, I was determined to find somewhere else to stay during the summer. I could not stay in my mother's house and be exposed to that toxic environment when I was so close to escaping. I spent the summer working to build up savings for room and board in Boston since my scholarship only covered tuition, fees, and books. I had several friends who graciously allowed me to "couch surf" the final two months before I departed for Boston University. I had arranged for an apartment in Boston with three other students so we could afford rent. I also had a part-time job set up when I got to Boston so I could sustain myself and finish school.

I started Boston University in early September 1983, and I was busy with a full load of classes, working twenty hours a week, and participating in Air Force ROTC. I found myself once again focused on my work, which in hindsight was my way of coping with the recent tragedies. The fog was heavy and I was feeling very alone. I managed to find comfort, or escape, in accomplishing my schoolwork and my increased responsibility as a ROTC cadet officer. The fall semester drew to a close and I was looking forward to the holiday break after finals. During this time, I had very little contact with my mother or other family members, and I would learn once I got home that my mother had sold her house. She decided there were too many memories and downsized into a small two-bedroom condo in another city. I learned that most of the stuff that was left in my room went to charity and there was a box with some of my stuff in my mother's garage. I went to visit my mother and collect my things and she offered me one of the bedrooms in her condo for the holiday break. My holiday plans were not set and I was staying with friends. I hoped this new environment would bring some welcome changes, so I agreed to stay with her for the holidays.

The condo my mother had bought was very nice for her and I hoped she would find strength to change. Quietly, I had blamed my mother for the terrible environment we lived in and how it had contributed to the death of my sister. We agreed to get along for the holidays and generally she was pleasant. I stayed well out of the way when the drinking started and managed to be out most of the time or risk an unpleasant encounter.

One evening, while we were both at the condo, there was a knock on the door. I stood up and said, "I will get it, Mom."

I opened the door and saw two local police officers standing there. Immediately, I had flashbacks to the old house where this was a common occurrence and I wondered what we had done wrong.

One of the officers said, "Sorry for the intrusion, but we are trying to locate Dorothy Faber. Does she live here?"

"Yes," I said. "That is my mother, and she just recently moved here. I am her son, Jim."

"Can we speak with both of you please?" the officer added.

"Mom," I yelled, "There are two officers here that want to speak with us."

My mother came to the door and the officer started, "Ma'am, is your son Albert Faber?"

"Yes," my mother replied. "What is going on?"

"Ma'am," the officer said, "I am sorry to inform you that your son has been killed in a car crash."

My mother lost it right on the spot and I suddenly felt all the blood rush from my head. *Are you kidding?* I thought to myself. I said, "How could this be? I was just with him earlier in the day. Are you certain it is Albie Faber?"

"Yes," the officer replied. "We had a positive ID by one of his friends at the morgue since we were unable to contact family. We had the old address and no phone number. The friend that ID'd him gave us this address."

My younger brother was only nineteen and was trying to get things together. He worked hard and was known to smoke some weed and drink a bit. Alcohol and marijuana would later be confirmed as contributing factors in his car crash.

The officers then helped me move my mother back into the condo and get her seated. I was lost for words and could not believe a third tragedy in eleven months had struck our family. I called my older brother to tell him, and he came straight over to the condo.

As I was seeing the officers out, they called me outside. "Can we see you for a minute?"

The officer then explained that my brother had lost control of his car and was ejected. The coroner was still working on test results, but eyewitnesses confirmed that he was driving erratically. The officer added, "When he was ejected from the car, he was pinned and drug for several hundred feet."

The officer explained, "I just want you to know that the injuries are what we call 'extensive,' and it might be a good idea not to visit the morgue since we already had a positive ID."

"Thank you," I said, and the officers left.

I did not relay any of this to my mother, but my older brother was determined to go to the morgue to see his brother one last time. I told him what the officer said, and the only way he was ID'd was because he was wearing a leather jacket the friend had let him borrow. This did not stop my brother, so I went with him to the morgue but refused to go any further than the waiting room. Based on what my brother would eventually tell me, I am happy I never went in to see my brother.

We had a third funeral in eleven months and my brother was immediately cremated since there was not much left for a proper casket service. The fog thickened and began to choke me. I had just lost my younger brother, whom I loved very much. We were the closest of all the children. My brother and I were inseparable and only a year apart. I was devastated again and my wounds were very deep.

I would return to school and essentially never return home again. The environment we were raised in certainly contributed to the tragic loss of my brother and sister. I was even more determined to escape this toxic environment and focused even harder on the road ahead. These tragedies taught me a valuable lesson that has stayed with me my entire life. Every day is a gift and we need to live them to the fullest. Each of us gets caught up in the daily grind and sometimes we cannot avoid it, but always stay focused on finding some down time. I coined a phrase for my life that I call, "Rushing to Relax!"

We all work hard, but I have developed an ability to stay laser focused and get my work done as quickly as possible. Yes, there are times when we all must burn the oil twenty-four hours a day, but if this becomes the norm in our lives, we are missing the important things. Spend as much time doing what you love in the company of people you love. Stop often along the way to smell the roses.

Some People Are Stupid, but Not YOU, Because:

You understand that every day is a gift and we need to slow down and smell the roses and live life to the fullest.

Chapter 4
Staying on Course

I have been blessed, or cursed depending on your perspective, with an ability to have laser focus and always keep my goal or objective in front of me. Not everyone has this laser focus or even needs this skill to stay on course. The biggest thing we have to remember is to remain focused on the big picture or the "big crazy goal" we have for our lives. This does not mean that we cannot change the goals or take detours along the way, but ultimately, if you set a goal, you will need to apply some effort towards achieving it. I wish there was a simple formula and a "wishing well" where dreams come true, but that is pure fiction. In the real world, we need to work hard to achieve our goals. My point is that you can achieve ANY GOAL that you set your mind to despite what anyone else says. Goals do not have to be earth-shattering or monumental and can be as simple as I am going to finish my schooling or something similar. We all need to set goals that are right for us and amend them as we move along—but never talk yourself into NOT setting a goal because it seems crazy or unachievable.

The higher we set our goals, the farther we will ultimately go, even if we fall short of the initial goal. When I was in high school, there was a very cool airplane the Air Force had begun to develop and some of the initial photos and flight test data got me really excited. I am talking about the B-1A program, and I thought this new high-tech bomber was something right out of the future. I set a goal that someday I was going to fly this airplane. My dreams were shattered when the B-1A program was cancelled by President Jimmy Carter in the mid-seventies, but I stayed focused on the bigger goal of seeking an Air Force Commission and going to flight school. I was disappointed that the B-1A would not be developed, but this was not something within my control, and there were many other great jets in the Air Force inventory. In 1980, Ronald Reagan was elected President, and he began a military expansion and development program to counter the threat of the Soviet Union during the height of the cold war. Luckily for me, Reagan's military expansion also included a reinstatement of the B-1 program in the form of the Rockwell B-1B Bomber.

I graduated from college in 1985, which also marked the delivery of the first operational B-1B to the United States Air Force at Dyess AFB, Texas. I had received my commission and was headed to flight school on a mission to somehow end up flying B-1Bs. The reality of flight school hit me pretty hard and I was not at all prepared for how hard it was going to be. I remained committed to my goal and worked harder than I had ever done in my life. I thought college had been hard, but in comparison to flight school, it was a walk in the park. I managed to do well in flight school but was by no means at the very top of my class. Only the top 5 to 10 percent of my graduating class would be selected to fly the most advanced and desirable Air Force jets, like the B-1B. I was just outside the top 10 percent and unlikely to improve my ranking before graduation. It turned out that since the B-1B had only just become operational, the Air Force was selecting only senior and very experienced aviators to be the "initial cadre" flying the jet. In other words, the B-1B was not on the list of available choices for a young second lieutenant just graduating from flight school, top 10 percent or not!

I stayed focused on the B-1B and went to my flight commander to discuss my available choices and the best path towards a B-1B. My flight commander told me, "In order to get selected for the B-1B program, you will need at least one thousand flight hours in a major weapon system."

My flight commander continued, "Your best shot at getting into the B-1B program is to select another airplane assigned to the same command as the B-1B."

In other words, my flight commander said, "You should select an airframe which is already part of the Strategic Air Command inventory."

The other options were Tactical Air Command or Military Airlift Command, but most of the folks selected for the B-1B were coming from a previous bomber background with the Strategic Air Command. This was a detour to say the least, but I was determined and ultimately selected a B-52 as my first choice to gain the much needed bomber experience and stay within the Strategic Air Command.

I went to B-52 training right after flight school and studied hard so I could learn how to effectively employ a major weapon system. The B-52 training was great, and I really enjoyed my time at Castle, AFB, where we were paired with other students to form crews and flew together for the duration of the training. I still remain in touch with a few of my fellow classmates from that training and overall, it was a great experience. I graduated from B-52 training in the fall of 1986 and I selected what was then known as a "Northern Tier" assignment. Everyone in B-52s was required to do a "remote" Northern Tier assignment at least once, and I figured I would get it out of the way as a young and single lieutenant. This was the height of the Cold War and manned bombers were stationed at the most northerly locations in the United States on ready alert in case the Soviet Union decided to start War World III. I chose Loring Air Force Base at the very northern tip of Maine on the border with Canada, and only a short hop over the polar ice cap to enter Russian territory.

Loring AFB is not the most northern point in the contiguous United States, but it is certainly on the list, which makes it a very remote and cold place. I was committed to getting my Northern Tier assignment out of the way while logging much needed flight hours and bomber experience for the B-1B program. I recall when I left California for the drive across the country, I stopped at Edwards Air Force Base in southern California for gas and road supplies. The Air Force Test Center is located at Edwards Air Force Base, and unknown to me, they were in the middle of flight-testing the B-1B. As I stopped at the base gas station not far from the flight line, I glanced at the airplane ramp and was amazed to see a B-1B parked on the ramp not more than a hundred yards away. This was the first time I had seen the B-1B for real and I was very excited. The B-1B program was still a protected and classified program, and seeing the jet in person was a rare occurrence. I was overwhelmed with the beauty of the jet and how fast it looked just sitting on the ramp. The pictures and videos I had seen of the B-1B did not do the jet justice, and I was like a kid in a candy store trying to get as close as I could for a better view. I was travelling with my girlfriend at the time, now my wife, and I told her that someday I was going to fly that jet. I do not think she fully appreciated how committed I was to getting selected to the B-1B program, as it seemed like something so far away and nearly impossible. Seeing the jet for the first time really re-committed me to the goal of working hard and someday being competitive enough for selection to the B-1B program.

A few days later, I arrived at my first assignment at Loring Air Force Base, home of the 42nd Bomb Wing and the 69th Bomb Squadron. The 69th Bomb Squadron was flying B-52G Models and we had a significant alert role as the "Northern Watch" during the Cold War, in addition to training to defend what is known as the United Kingdom, Greenland, Iceland gap over the North Atlantic. The North Atlantic was considered essential for shipping lanes in case WWIII ever broke out, or another nation threatened these critical shipping and communication lanes between Europe and the United States. The 69th Bomb Squadron had a very large naval mission in addition to the traditional Cold War alert role, which involved learning how to deploy various types of sea mines, protecting shipping lanes, and employment of the anti-ship missile "Harpoon." The mission was important and played a critical role during the Cold War due to our proximity to the Polar Ice Cap and the short time it took to fly from Loring into Russian Airspace. To keep things interesting, we also had a full conventional mission that included various other weapons we could employ in a more traditional war. I was very excited to be at Loring and looked forward to learning how to employ the B-52G and the many roles that the 69th Bomb Squadron was tasked to perform.

I reported to my squadron commander and received the standard welcome briefing that included the commander's expectations of a young second lieutenant. "Sir," I started, "Lieutenant Faber reporting as ordered."

"At ease," my commander said. "Welcome to Loring Air Force Base, we are excited to have you here and look forward to getting you started right away."

"Yes sir," I said. "Very happy to be here and start my combat crew training."

Next my commander said, "Lieutenant Faber, I expect you to be the best B-52 navigator that ever set foot in the 69th Bomb Squadron. Excellence is the standard!"

"Yes sir," I replied.

This same speech was probably rehearsed and presented to every young officer reporting into the squadron, but it highlights the very competitive nature of the Air Force flying business. The notion that being the best aviator in the world was "the standard" really highlights that you had to make a name for yourself both inside and outside of the cockpit. I informed the commander that I was excited to be part of the 69th Bomb Squadron and that I was going to work very hard to be the best I could be and contribute to the mission of the squadron. The commander then asked me, "What are your goals while assigned here?"

Wow, I thought to myself, no one has ever asked me what my goals are. I replied, "Well sir, first and foremost, my primary focus is to learn the mission of the 69th and to pick up additional duties appropriate for a young lieutenant."

"OK," my commander responded, "anything else?"

"Yes sir," I replied, trying to sound confident but not cocky. "I have always wanted to fly the B-1B Bomber and want to make myself competitive for that program."

I worried my commander might start laughing or write me off for such a lofty goal, but being a good commander he said, "That is a lofty but solid goal, and although not available to you now as a junior officer, over time you may become eligible."

"I can promise you this," my commander said, "if you do well and work hard in the squadron while logging the required flight hours, I will support your effort to get accepted into the B-1B flight program."

My heart missed a beat when my commander said he would support my goal! I was very pleased with our meeting and with renewed energy, motivation, and commitment, set out to be the best B-52 navigator in the 69th Bomb Squadron.

I was assigned to a B-52 crew and one of the most senior radar navigators (RN), or bombardiers, in the squadron. It was his job to ensure I was progressing as a young bomber navigator. In the B-52, there are two navigators located on the lower deck of the cockpit. The more senior navigator is designated the radar navigator (RN) and is responsible for target acquisition and weapons delivery. My job was to get us to the target within plus or minus three seconds of our scheduled time on target, and essentially plan the entire mission from takeoff through landing. It was a challenging job and in the late 1980s we did not have GPS and high-tech radars, so the job really tested your skill. I was responsible for all of the weapons payload along with the RN, and we worked as a close-knit team managing the sortie, conducting rendezvous with the airborne tanker, changing course to make our strict target times, and assigning and arming weapons for each target. A typical B-52 sortie was action packed from takeoff to landing and you were always working to stay ahead of the jet.

My RN and I worked OK as a team, but we definitely had a personality conflict and never spent any time together when we were off duty. My RN was a screamer and had nothing but negative things to say about my performance, even when I had not made any mistakes. I am not motivated by screamers and negative feedback, so I learned early in my career to "salute smartly and carry on," and this helped me survive these types of individuals. I mention this because I could have gotten discouraged by the negative energy from my RN, but instead, I worked even harder to learn and employ all the weapons of the 69th Bomb Squadron. In addition, I also signed up for a bunch of extra duties that no one else wanted, ranging from targeteering work in the weapons shop, updating and putting together mission packages for our sorties, becoming the Wing expert and trainer for a complicated weapons delivery formula that every navigator had to master, and becoming the air show narrator and key planner.

I spent about a year on my first crew with the screamer and was beginning to make a name for myself. I had already upgraded to instructor navigator with the minimum amount of hours and had also been selected for a new Conventional Strike Program where I was upgraded as one of three flight lead instructor navigators from a group of about twenty-five navigators. The squadron was putting together select crews that could act as flight leads, and I was recruited to join another crew as the new flight lead. It ended up being the opportunity that really helped me advance in the squadron. My new radar navigator was the senior-most RN in the squadron. He personally asked me to join his crew, and together we would eventually take top honors in the squadron as the number one crew. I enjoyed my time with this new RN who was very tough, but fair, and didn't use negative feedback as a motivational technique. Under his leadership, I really matured as a B-52 navigator and was being selected for the highest visibility missions and deployments. The flying side of things was going well, but as previously mentioned, being the best aviator was the standard and I was gaining traction with my additional duties. My work in the weapons shop helped them win a few awards for excellence, and my time dedicated to the airshow was highlighting me as the face of the 42nd Bomb Wing at one of our most important and visible public events.

I was approaching my second year in the 69th Bomb Squadron and was one of the senior instructor navigators. The Air Force announced it was going to start selections for the B-1B program and a list of eligibility requirements were published. I still needed more flight hours, and I also needed more time in my squadron before becoming eligible to apply. I went to see my commander, whom I reported into nearly two years earlier, and asked him if there was any way I could apply for the B-1B program and seek a waiver for the flight hours and time on station requirements. The commander was a man of his word, and when he said if I worked hard in the squadron, he would support my effort to get into the B-1B program, that is what he did. My commander approached the 42nd Bomb wing commander, who knew me from my role as the air show narrator and work as the Wing trainer for the weapons delivery formula. The wing commander said that he was inclined to support my request for a waiver. I put together the waiver package for the wing commander and he fully supported my effort, resulting in an approved waiver from Air Force headquarters for both the time on station and the flight time requirements!

The waiver was the first step, and it allowed me to assemble and submit a full nominating package to the B-1B selection board. I was not certain how many aviators applied to the B-1B Selection Board, and I knew that only a few were selected in my aviation specialty each year due to limited space in the startup B-1B training program. I received an initial message from the B-1B board that they had accepted my waiver with one condition. IF I was selected to join the B-1B program, the board would require me to stay at the 69th Bomb Squadron and get the additional flight time required so that I had at least one thousand hours in the B-52. I gladly signed the agreement letter so that I would be considered. In reality, I was only a few hundred hours shy of one thousand. I knew that by the time the board made their decision and I was assigned a class date, I would probably have all the required hours.

It was January 1989 and the B-1B Board had begun releasing results for the upcoming training year. Since the program was so new, there were only about four classes offered each year, with just four students in each class. A few more senior aviators in my squadron were notified they had been selected and had late winter class start dates. A few others had start dates in the spring. As the winter progressed, I was beginning to think that I was too young in my career and that the board would not select me in the current cycle. I had resigned myself that I would need to reapply for the next year since most of the class dates had already been announced and everyone selected were more senior officers with much more flying time than I had.

In April, I was called into my commander's office to talk about an upcoming squadron deployment to the United Kingdom that I was planning. Our conversation was about the details of the deployment and the missions we would be flying while in Europe. As I was leaving the commander's office, he said, "Lieutenant Faber, one more thing."

I turned around and replied, "Yes Sir?"

My commander pulled out a folder and told me he had the results of the latest B-1B Board. I could feel my heart skip a beat. He was taking his time, and I feared the news was not good. He looked up from the folder holding a piece of paper and said, "Congratulations, Lieutenant Faber, you have been selected for the B-1B program!"

I stood there in a state of disbelief, for suddenly a goal and dream that I had been pursuing for over fourteen years was finally about to come true. My commander then informed me that I was also the youngest officer at the time to have been selected for the B-1B program. He told me that I had an early fall class date and I needed to sign and return the acceptance letter within twenty-four hours, accepting or declining the assignment to make it official. It did not take me more than twenty-four seconds to sign the official acceptance letter!! I was going to fly the newest and most advanced airplane in the Air Force inventory, realizing a dream and goal I had set over a decade earlier.

Some People Are Stupid, but Not YOU, Because:

You understand that a continued laser focus on your life's biggest goals will help you achieve much more than if you had never set such a high goal in the first place, despite a few detours along the way.

Chapter 5
A Life of Service

"Service Before Self" is an Air Force motto I adopted for my life many years ago. I have always been in the service of others and by no means have I done it well, but I have always tried to serve others in everything I do. My view is that we are only passing through and what we are able to leave behind is the most valuable of possessions that any of us can pass on. I have fallen short on many occasions but still endeavor every day to be of service in some small way. I have been very fortunate in my life to make a few career choices that resulted in the juxtaposition of service to others and making a living. According to renowned American psychologist Abraham Maslow's "Hierarchy of Needs," we each strive throughout our lives to achieve harmony and our full potential, or as Maslow refers to it, "becoming self-actualized."

Of course, none of us are perfect and achieving self-actualization is more of a journey than a set destination. Becoming "self-actualized" will look different for everyone and there is no "aha moment" announcing that you have arrived, but generally, it occurs when each of us has achieved our fullest potential. To me, reaching our full potential may change as we mature, but always working towards it and living a life of service before self keeps us headed in the right direction. Service before self is about leaving this world just a little better than when we found it.

I am no saint and did not intend to spend my life in service to others, but it sort of happened that way. And once I realized the path I was on, I pursued it with all my passion. We are not always in control of our path in life as much as we think we are. We work hard and set goals, but as I have said previously, there are always unplanned detours and different paths that present themselves along the way. The path I pursued initially was the Air Force, and I admit my initial reason for seeking a commission was to fly the most advanced jets in the world. As I pursued my AF career, I realized that this was more than simply flying cool jets. It was a real calling to serve others and support and defend the Constitution of the United States. The Oath of Office when I was commissioned really helped me understand the gravity of the appointment and my commitment to give my life, if required, in support of the US Constitution and ultimately to protect the American way of life.

In flight school, I knew I wanted to be a combat crewmember and at the time the US was at the height of the Cold War. As a combat crewmember on B-52s in Strategic Air Command, I would find myself at the very pointy end of the spear during the Cold War as we stared down the Russians with the promise of Mutually Assured Destruction (MAD).

If we had a World War III, my mission to defend the United States was pretty much a one-way trip, but none of us balked or had any issue with that sacrifice to protect the United States. I can recall sitting alert with a fully loaded bomber for seven days at a time about every third week for the first six years of my career as a combat crewmember. It was our job to be on "ready-alert" in case the Russians decided to launch, or threaten to launch, an attack on the United States, a thought that today seems quite distant and absurd. The reality during the Cold War was much more serious and there were several episodes between the United States and Russia that are well documented by historians where we came much closer to a nuclear war than most Americans ever fully realized. I am not going to discuss particular episodes or speculate further, since I may start to delve into areas I am not at liberty to discuss, but understand that the men and woman sitting alert around the globe and making great sacrifices held the Russians at bay and prevented WWIII from ever happening. This was a "calling" to serve others and perhaps make the ultimate sacrifice, much like Americans have done for generations and continue to do today. The Cold War "officially" ended in 1991 and I was pleased to take one of the last B-1B Bombers off alert and felt proud of all that Strategic Air Command had done. I, along with many other dedicated professionals across agencies, put service before self to prevent the "unthinkable" from ever happening.

My service in the Air Force would eventually span just a bit longer than twenty years and there were numerous deployments, assignments, and conflicts that would place many others and myself in harm's way defending the American Way of Life. After twenty years, I retired and decided I would try the civilian sector and specifically the "for-profit" world. I enjoyed my experience in the "for-profit" world and I was making very good money, but for me, something was missing. I do not begrudge anyone who works hard and earns a large income, but I need to be connected to some mission or greater good to feel like what I do matters. Plenty of my friends are very wealthy and I am happy they have been able to pursue their interests and earn small fortunes. That, after all, is the American Way and I am proud to be able to say that in a small way, I contributed to the safety and security that has enabled them to earn their fortunes. For me, the earning of a large salary or closing a deal for the sake of getting it done to increase shareholder and company value is simply not motivating. I applaud all those that do find great satisfaction in these things and wish them well, since a strong US economy coupled with a strong military is the best way to protect and preserve America's leadership role in the world today.

After a few years in the "for-profit" sector, I was fortunate enough to be hired as a CEO for a medium-sized non-profit that served over twenty thousand clients annually. The non-profit had a long track record of serving others across a variety of "poverty reduction" programs, and we were making a real difference in the lives of many individuals and families. The work was hard and securing funding to keep the work moving forward was a constant challenge. I was very passionate about the mission to help people "learn to fish" and create their own version of the American Dream by getting specific technical job training, an advanced education, buying a first home, or starting their own small business. I never minded the long hours we worked to ensure the organization was well funded, and we had quite a few success stories along the way that kept me and my staff motivated to continue serving others. I was so passionate about our mission having my own story of coming "up from poverty" that my team was able to increase revenue streams significantly and grow and expand our programs to serve thousands more clients. I was happy in this work, and although I was not making the kind of money I could make in the for-profit sector, I felt self-actualized. I would add that although I was not making insane amounts of money in this work, I was fairly compensated and, along with my military retirement, was leading a comfortable life with my wife and four children. I am truly blessed to have had this opportunity where mission was far more important than dollars earned.

I served as the CEO for the non-profit for about five and a half years and then retired again to find the next area of service. I still had great passion for the work of the non-profit, but felt I had accomplished all that I could and a change of leadership with fresh ideas would be best for the mission. The organization was in a great place financially and organizationally, so I felt it was time to hand it over to someone else that could take it to the next level. My board was not happy with my decision to retire after only five years, but they understood that I needed a new and different challenge. To this day I remain thankful to my board of directors for being so graceful and understanding of my need to find the next place to serve. As fate would have it, my next opportunity came from a friend that I knew from over fifteen years of volunteering together to run one of the largest annual single-day fundraisers in our local community. My friend was a firefighter and, along with his fire station, had donated thousands of man-hours and money supporting this very important fundraiser. One day, while we were working to set up for the fundraiser, I asked him about the medical side of firefighting. He explained what firefighters do regarding medical calls and that many, if not all, the firefighters had at least an Emergency Medical Technician (EMT) national certification.

I learned about the EMT career field and was quite impressed by all the training and medical skills that these EMTs had and their responsibility as medical first responders. I quickly realized this was another area where "Service Before Self" was clearly the driving force of why these brave men and women would rush into a potentially dangerous situation to help another human being. These men and women put their own safety at risk to help anyone injured or sick. They responded to countless medical emergencies, ranging from traumatic accidents to a myriad of medical emergencies such as strokes, heart attacks, difficulty breathing and way beyond. I was hooked and asked my friend, "How can I help and what training is required to earn this certification?"

He replied, "Jim, this is a real commitment and will require a lot of your time and about a year of training."

I then learned my friend's fire station was offering an EMT course and that I could join the course and eventually be prepared to sit for the national exam. I did not hesitate and signed up for the course and really enjoyed learning anatomy and physiology, pharmacology, patient assessment and all of the many skills we had at our disposal to potentially save someone's life.

I completed the course, passed my national certification and was fortunate to be hired shortly thereafter with a national ambulance company that handled the local contract in Colorado Springs. I was sent to their academy to learn about the operation, our medical protocols, the equipment carried on the ambulance, and to earn my IV certification.

During the first day of the academy, we were all introducing ourselves and when I explained I was a retired AF lieutenant colonel, a successful entrepreneur, and retired non-profit CEO, one of my classmates turned and simply asked, "Why are you here?"

I replied that it was about "service before self and I wanted to continue serving others in some way."

I was not doing it for the paycheck, that is for certain, and without starting another chapter, most Americans would be shocked at how little many of the medical first responders (Paramedics and EMTs) earn compared to their level of training and responsibility! Since working for this ambulance company, I have completed my field training and am "cleared" to work part-time as my schedule allows or as I am needed. I can say that when I arrive on scene, which is possibly the worst day of someone's life, I am happy to be there to assist them and comfort them as my life of service continues.

Some People Are Stupid, but Not YOU, Because:

You understand that what matters the most in our lives is what we have done for others and the legacy we leave behind.

Chapter 6
Karma

I am a firm believer in treating others as I want to be treated, and throughout my life I have tried to live up to this principle. Have I missed the mark a few times and made mistakes? You bet! In every case where I missed the mark, I would ultimately pay for it one way or another and was constantly reminded to do better the next time. I watched several colleagues and friends throughout my career that never quite figured this out, and they wondered why they did not get the next promotion, or land that great job, or seemed to be living under a dark cloud. I am far from perfect and sometimes find it really hard to be nice to certain people, but I always try.

When I was coming up through the ranks in the Air Force, there was always someone with more rank and experience that acted like a complete jerk. I saw this in the civilian world as well, so it is not isolated to the military by a long shot. When I was a young second lieutenant, I showed up at flight school at Mather, AFB in Sacramento, California. The flight training was difficult and I had to study a lot for the concepts to sink in. The flight instructors were generally good people, and all of them had several thousand flight hours in a major weapon system and were coming back to train the new guys. The attrition rate in flight school was fairly high due to the complexity of learning to navigate and fly. There were "those" instructors who were mid-level captains, or young majors that had serious attitude problems. It seemed that their sole purpose was to flunk you out of flight school, not actually instruct or teach you anything. Please understand that all the instructors were very hard and demanding and expected top performance, but most of them were fair. The great instructors were the ones that taught you something and allowed you enough rope to get into trouble but never too much to jeopardize safety or the mission. Then there were the other instructors that must have been seriously abused when they were in flight school and perhaps thought it was a rite of passage to abuse the new guys. These instructors were the screamers and on your case about every little detail, never really giving you the opportunity to make corrections. I never learned anything from these instructors and just endeavored to survive them. I vowed that if I were ever to become a flight instructor I would be firm, expect excellence, and be fair with my students. I never have seen the need to be cruel, or abuse a position of power simply because you can, and in all honesty, I saw this way too much among the flight instructors. Of course, if you were the one to say something, back in my day, you would be the first to be driving off the base having "legitimately failed" flight training.

While in flight school, I was assigned to a flight that consisted of about twenty students and a flight commander who was also a flight instructor. I am uncertain if this was a rule, but flight commanders did not often fly with students from their own flight. It might have been due to the competition between flights for "Top Honors," and grading one of your own students might be a conflict of interest. Not certain if this was true, but it was good enough for me and I never actually flew with my flight commander. However, I did spend an enormous amount of extra time with my flight commander learning flight procedures, studying missions, and asking questions about everything. One could say that this was his job, but he often stayed late to work extra with me and any other students that needed additional help, whether they were in his flight or not. This must have been a great burden for him, since the only time we could see him was after hours because the days were full with classes and flights. My flight commander was also very busy during the day dealing with the administration of the flight in addition to carrying a full instruction load. My flight commander was married and had children, but gave up almost every evening to work with any student needing help and many times came in on weekends as well. I learned a great deal about flying from him, but most importantly, I learned what a great instructor looked like. He was firm, demanded our top performance, did not tolerate incompetence due to a lack of effort or knowledge, was understanding when we made mistakes and allowed us to make them, was a very professional officer/aviator, and had tremendous humility. If only I could be half as good someday.

I would ultimately graduate from flight school, get my wings and go on to specialty training to learn how to fly my specific weapons system. I thanked my flight commander for everything he had done and presented him with a gift from our class as a small token of our appreciation. I left Mather, AFB, and lost track of my flight commander as I transitioned into my career. About six years passed since I had been in flight school and I was a mid-level captain flying B-1Bs and things had been going well. I was selected to attend Central Flight Instructor School or CFIC to become a B-1B flight instructor and I was excited and honored. I showed up for CFIC and was very eager to spend several weeks studying and learning the B-1B systems in much more depth so I could be an effective instructor. While in CFIC, you actually fly with an instructor (yes, an instructor of instructors!) who pretends to be a new B-1B student and tries to make all the mistakes a typical student makes, and then some. It is very challenging, since you really have to have an in-depth knowledge of all the jet's systems and stay several steps ahead of your student anticipating what is coming next to ensure flight safety and mission accomplishment.

During CFIC, the "instructors in training" are eventually paired up with actual B-1B students since the base was also home to B-1B initial qualification training. Most of the students were young lieutenants, just like I was several years before when I completed flight school. This was their first time in a truly high-performance jet, flying in a very busy tactical environment while learning to employ the weapon system at speeds at or near the speed of sound. A challenging and exciting time at the least, and definitely fun and rewarding if you did the work. Of course, there were also students that were more senior and were transitioning into the B-1B from another weapon system. We had many students transitioning from other weapons systems like the F-111, B-52, F-4, and several non-tactical airframes like airlift, tankers, reconnaissance, and many other specialty aircraft.

CFIC was going along well, and I had already flown a few sorties with my instructor, or pretend student. I had been working very hard and caught most of the mistakes he intentionally made before they became serious issues, but I still had a lot to learn. It was decided that I was ready for a "real" student and was given the specifics of the mission, where the student was in his initial B-1B training, and where to meet for the pre-flight mission planning the next day. I was very excited and spent the night before reviewing all the goals and performance measures required for the upcoming training sortie. I studied all of my instructor manuals, techniques, and what I had already learned, and was determined not to become a "screamer." I wanted to assist my student while allowing him to learn from his mistakes in a safe and positive-reinforcing environment.

The next day, I showed up at the appointed time and place to meet my student and prepare for the upcoming sortie. I walked into the briefing room and was completely surprised to see my flight commander from when I was a young lieutenant in flight school. I had not seen him for six years and I was pleased to spend a few minutes catching up on what he had been doing since leaving Mather, AFB. I asked him what he was doing there, and he stated, "I am transitioning into the B-1B weapon system and will be retuning to a combat squadron after having just completed a staff tour."

"Wait a minute," I said. "You are my student?"

I had no idea who my student was going to be on this day, and as fate would have it, the student (me six years earlier) had become the instructor! I was a bit overwhelmed at first, since I thought he had been one of the best instructors I ever had, and now I was his instructor. I remained professional and started working with him on the next day's sortie, very determined to be as helpful to him as he was to me six years earlier. I would have been very professional and helpful to any student assigned to me, even if it was one of the awful "screamers" from flight school, but it was nice it to work with someone I admired so much.

I worked very hard with my former flight commander, who was a major at this point, as we reviewed and "Chair Flew" the entire sortie so that he was very well prepared. I went over all the standard procedures with him and shared several great techniques I had learned over the past three years flying the B-1B. I stayed as long as he wanted that night, and he asked a ton of questions about the sortie, the B-1B systems, and picked my brain on almost everything else. I was happy to go the extra mile for him, and as time would eventually tell, this would become my standard operating procedure as a B-1B flight instructor. Had it been one of the terrible instructors from when I was a flight student, I certainly would have gone the extra mile for them as well, but if I am being perfectly honest, it would not have felt as good. We flew the sortie the next day and my old flight commander did a fabulous job, with a few minor issues here and there, but overall was excellent. I felt proud that I was able to "give back" to him just a little for what he did for me. He had lived the motto, "Treat others like you want to be treated," and it came back around. After we debriefed the sortie, he leaned over and said, "You have matured into a really great flight instructor." Wow!!

Some People Are Stupid, but Not YOU, Because:

You treat other people the way you want to be treated to avoid having negative karma come back and haunt you. It's really true,
"What goes around, comes around."

Chapter 7
Pass It On

I have talked in a previous story about karma and "what goes around, comes around," but what is equally important is remembering to show the same grace to others as you were shown at some earlier point in your life. Many people tend to forget parts of the road they travelled and when it is their turn to mentor, instruct, lead, or similar, they fail to recall that someone along the line gave them a break. We have all received a break along the way in some small form or another and I think it is important to recognize that it really does "take a village" to continually improve and become better people. I know I certainly had a break or two along the way, some deserved and some by the sheer grace of God, but nonetheless they happened and I always try to keep that in mind when I am in a position of leadership or influence.

When I was in flight school in 1985, I had my challenges and spent a lot of time studying. However, there was always a concept or two that I had a hard time translating into practice. I had been doing OK, staying up with my class, and learning a great deal about flying, when I encountered a concept that gave me some trouble. One of the things you do while flying is always to maintain "situational awareness" of what is going on inside the cockpit, but, more importantly, where the airplane is at any given time. In basic flight school, we were not allowed the use of advanced avionics (GPS, inertial navigation systems, Doppler for drift correction and groundspeed) and were required to manually compute these critical navigational elements.

In order to compute the critical elements of navigation, one would keep a running time, speed, course, and correct for wind to make the next navigation point within the prescribed time parameters. The process of keeping track of the airplane and marking spots on the map is called "dead reckoning" and having a good "DR" was very important to determine where you were at a given point in time. Based on your running "DR," you would make course corrections as needed to stay or correct back to the planned course. The process of keeping a running "DR" is very simple once you figure out a few elements of the navigational puzzle (essentially time, distance, and speed). However, if you make a mistake along the way, the problem can compound if left uncorrected. If your first "DR" is off when you place it on the map and you use that as a good position, then the next "DR" about twenty minutes later is going to be off as well, and so it goes until you realize your mistake, or you are truly lost. On my check ride, which is kind of like a final exam in this phase of flight school, my "DR" plots on my map were outside of the accepted tolerances due to an initial plotting error. I never caught the initial error and the problem was compounded. I failed this important check ride and was rescheduled to do the ride again, or face elimination from flight school.

I showed up for my rescheduled check ride and, as you might imagine, I was a bit nervous since this could mean the end of my Air Force flying career. Up until this point, I had been doing just fine in flight school and never even thought I would come close to washing out, but my reality was suddenly altered. I prepared diligently for the check ride and felt confident I could pass the second time around. I showed up for the pre-flight briefing and my assigned instructor for the flight was a naval flight officer, a Navy lieutenant which is the equivalent of an Air Force captain, on exchange with the Air Force. We briefed the mission and my naval flight instructor put me at ease and said, "Just relax and do your job and everything will turn out just fine."

"Yes sir," I replied.

I really appreciated his grace and understanding since I was already under a lot of pressure and he did not need to add to it. The flight was fairly straightforward and I felt comfortable with the mission. We launched on a late afternoon sortie and would fly into the early evening watching the California sunset on our return to base. Everything was going well on the flight and I was maintaining great situational awareness, a solid "DR," and felt in control of the flight. My evaluator hardly said a thing during the flight, which is typically a very good sign. The less an evaluator says on a check ride typically means you are doing well, and the more they say to input corrections or flight safety issues translates into a failing check ride. We completed the sortie, and I knew I had a great flight and felt very confident as we shut down the jet and headed into the squadron for our debriefing.

My instructor started the debrief by announcing it was his anniversary, and since it was getting late, that he needed to take his wife to dinner and would I mind if we debriefed in the morning. I quickly replied, "Not at all sir, I am happy to debrief in the morning."

My heart sank a bit because I just wanted to know if I had passed the check ride. All the details of a full debrief could certainly wait, and quite frankly, once I knew I had passed, anything else my instructor had said would have been lost in the haze of my excitement that I would get to stay in flight school. My instructor understood this very well and said, "Don't worry, you did a great job and have nothing to worry about."

Breathing a sigh of relief I replied, "Thank you very much sir, I really appreciate it!"

As we were saying our goodbyes, my instructor mentioned in passing that there was a small area of the flight that we would discuss in detail in the morning, but not to worry since it was minor and he simply wanted to help me get better at this aspect of flying to help me as I progressed through flight school. I asked him what the issue was so that I could review and be prepared for the debriefing. He said, "Not a big deal, but two of your 'DRs' were slightly out of the accepted tolerances."

I began to quietly panic as it suddenly became clear that my instructor did not recall why I had to do the check ride over again. In the Air Force flight program, you are graded as having met standards on each check ride and you cannot regress in any area or it becomes an automatic failure outside the control of the instructor. In other words, I had received a "Below Performance Rating" in "DR" on my initial check ride, meaning I could not get another "Below" rating in that category or I would automatically fail and be kicked out of flight school.

My instructor looked at me and said, "Let me review the sortie tonight and look at this carefully and we can talk in the morning."

In my mind, his hands were tied, and this was an automatic failure. I was very upset, as I knew my Air Force flying career was over. The next morning, I met my instructor for the debriefing and figured that after he had reviewed the sortie and grading standards the night before, he had realized his hands were tied. I had accepted the fact I would be leaving flight school as the debriefing started and what happened next was an amazing act of grace that caught me completely off guard.

My instructor started the debriefing by saying, "Only two of your 'DRs' were slightly out of tolerance, and you made timely corrections that never significantly impacted the mission."

He went on to say, "I have to look at the bigger picture and the overall mission and ask myself: Does this young lieutenant have the ability to be successful flying high-performance jets similar to what I have done in the Navy?"

His answer was a simple, "Yes, you can successfully perform at this level and do not deserve to be sent home!"

I was excited, and a bit puzzled, since the grading standards are very strict and I did not see a way around them. He simply stated, "You deserve to be here, and some arbitrary grading standard for a relatively minor aspect of the flight should not be a reason to send you home."

He wrote the grade sheet to explain how the sortie went and simply avoided the details of the minor errors and wrote a statement saying that, "Lieutenant Faber had a very strong check ride and will be a very successful Air Force Aviator, retain in flight program."

I had been given one of the biggest breaks of my life and my dream was kept alive, strangely enough by the Navy, for which I am forever grateful. I went on to graduate and received my wings several months later with no other setbacks and went on to have a very successful Air Force flying career.

The story does not end there. After having flown B-52 and B-1Bombers, I found myself as a flight instructor nearly ten years later. I had heard of a new joint flight-training program that was going to start combining Air Force flight school with the Navy and Marine Corps flying programs. The new program had not yet started and was slated to begin at the Naval Air Station located at Pensacola, Florida. My timing was right, since I was at a point in my career where I needed to do what the Air Force calls an "Alpha tour" for aviators. An Alpha tour for me could consist of being a B-1B flight instructor at Dyess AFB, Texas, an air liaison officer attached to an Army battalion, or a basic flight instructor at one of several Air Force flight programs. The Air Force was not yet "hiring" instructors for the new joint Navy, Marine Corps, Air Force flight training program, but that did not stop me in persisting and learning all I could about the program.

I convinced my squadron commander that I would really prefer to help start a new flight training program rather than any of the other options, but the assignment folks had not yet created the billets for the program. I was told I would be headed to Dyess AFB to be a B-1B flight instructor at the schoolhouse. But I was already a B-1B flight instructor and had logged hundreds of instructor hours at my current B-1B squadron and wanted a different challenge. I persisted and kept working with the assignment folks and ended up finding the point of contact with the Air Training Command that was the lead in starting the joint flying training. My persistence paid off. Eventually, the Air Force announced the joint flying training program, and I was selected as the first Air Force flight instructor assigned to Navy Squadron VT-10 at Navy Pensacola to help establish the program.

My assignment with the Navy was great and I really enjoyed instructing basic flight students in the ways of low level visual navigation, high level instrument work, and all the basics of navigation and weapons systems. At about the two-year mark into my three-year assignment, I became one of the senior instructors and evaluators at the training wing and was selected for promotion to a senior evaluator position. I was selected as one of only two instructors in the whole wing of about 350 instructors as a "Special Progress Check" evaluator, known as a SPROG instructor. A SPROG instructor was the last resort before a student was kicked out of flight school and SPROG check rides could only take place at the request of the wing commander, or commodore as the Navy refers to them.

All students facing elimination could request a final review and appeal with the commodore if they felt their case warranted special attention. Many students met with the commodore, who then upheld the decisions of the squadron instructors to "wash-out" the student after many attempts had been made to bring them up to standards. It is actually quite a fair process and it becomes very apparent which students simply are not meant to fly and are sent on to do other things. In some cases, the commodore cannot quite decide and feels a particular student deserves one more chance, and that is where the SPROG instructors come in. I will highlight that SPROG check rides were not that common and the commodore did not use them often. But when he did, only myself or one other instructor was allowed to fly with the student. Once the commodore made the decision to give a student a "SPROG check" as it was called, the decision then resided solely and exclusively with the SPROG instructor with no further recourse from the student and no further action allowed by the commodore. This was quite a responsibility, since you had the final word on whether a young lieutenant or ensign would remain in flight school or go home.

I was called into the commodore's office, where he told me he had a young Marine lieutenant he was not quite certain about and wanted to give him one last chance. I saluted smartly, grabbed the student's flight folder, and then proceeded to schedule the SPROG check for the very next day. I informed the student the commodore gave him one last chance and that the flight the next day could be any mission he was comfortable with as long as it met the minimum requirements for a standard check ride in the particular phase of training. The Marine second lieutenant was excited, and very nervous to have the opportunity to prove himself and hopefully stay in the flight program. We met for the pre-flight briefing early the next day. He was a very squared away young Marine officer and really did a good job covering all the required aspects of the briefing and the flight details.

I started the preflight meeting by trying to put him at ease. "Lieutenant, I really want you to relax and do your best," I said. "Do not put any additional pressure on yourself and don't worry about me, just fly the sortie."

"Yes sir,' the lieutenant replied. "Thank you very much, sir. I really want to be here and will focus solely on doing my best."

When he was done briefing the mission, I explained to him the special nature of the SPROG check: that there were no further appeals from this point and the decision was 100 percent mine. I then explained, "There will be no grade sheet for this sortie and I will not be talking during the flight or offering any assistance, unless there is a safety of flight issue."

"Just fly the sortie," I continued. "Try to forget I am even there."

I assured him that all he had to do was his job and not worry about anything else, which, I hoped, put him somewhat at ease. At the end of the flight, I would then make a determination about whether he stayed in flight school or went home; simple as that.

We flew the sortie, which consisted of several difficult mission elements, and honestly, I was not blown away by his performance. He made several procedural errors during the mission and a few other mistakes that, on a normal check ride, would have earned him a downgrade and possibly a failure. I watched him closely and understood the pressure he was under. Despite all of that, he managed to function pretty well. The mistakes he made were due to his limited flight experience and the pressure of the flight itself. I thought long and hard after the sortie about his performance and asked myself one simple question: Can this young lieutenant do in the Marine Corps what I did in the Air Force and fly high performance jets?

Although not a perfect sortie, I recalled he was a student just learning and that none of the mistakes he made threatened the safety of the aircraft or hurt the mission. When we landed, I told him that he deserved to be in flight school and should be retained in the program. He thanked me profusely and was very excited and I told him, "You earned it!"

This lieutenant would go on to graduate several months later and eventually end up having a very long and successful career in the Marine Corps flying F-18D fighters and logging combat hours years later in the wake of 9/11.

At the time this occurred, I had not really thought much about my similar experience in flight school ten years earlier and how it was a Naval officer that saved my career. How ironic that I, an Air Force officer, would save the career of a Naval/Marine flight officer ten years later. I was pleased to be invited to his graduation ceremony and help present him with his set of Naval Wings. To commemorate the SPROG check, the young lieutenant presented me with my own set of Gold Naval Wings during his graduation, engraved on the back with our names and the date of the SPROG check. This remains one of my most prized possessions to this day.

<u>Some People Are Stupid, but Not YOU, Because:</u>

You understand that you should treat others with the same grace you were given in your career and life.

Chapter 8
Rules

This is a chapter about the rules and laws that are in place from the federal, state, and local levels that are designed to preserve order in our society while at the same time protecting our freedoms. I will begin by agreeing that some rules and laws that exist are pretty silly and many of them get modified to reflect the current "mood" or general advances in our society and culture. The rules and laws that have withstood the test of time remain in place simply because they help protect our freedoms and maintain some semblance of order to allow our diverse republic to function. Many people fail to remember that liberty and freedom are rights we have earned over the years through sacrifices large and small. We all give up some of our liberty and freedom to have a civil and ordered society that is safe and allows us to pursue our own version of the American Dream.

I can stand in one place and swing my arms in circles all day long if I choose, but that right is immediately revoked if one of my swinging arms just happens to connect with someone else's face, or violates their personal space. This is a very simple example, but most rules exist to keep us safe or to create an orderly environment for us all to operate in. Standing in line is one example of a "rule" that you wait in an orderly fashion for the doors to open or whatever it is you and others are waiting for. I admit that some rules seem a bit trivial, but I observe them all the same, since they apply to everyone and it is about the bigger picture. We are all subject to the same rules if we are in the same place and I am no better than you, so I comply out of respect for our civil order, our liberties, and my fellow citizens. So why then, are there people who believe that the rules do not apply to them?

We see people every day deciding that some rules are for everyone else, but not them. I see examples on a daily basis and wonder what these people are thinking and what would happen if we all were just a bit more respectful towards one another. As an example, my youngest two children attend a school that has a very strict drop-off and pickup procedure to ensure that the children are safe and do not get run over by another parent dropping off their children. The school was built in a strange location and has very limited access and no frontage road. In order to drop off and pick up your children, the school has devised a very detailed plan that would make NASA proud. At the beginning of the school year, there is often confusion as parents "relearn" the procedures, but after a week or two, the drop-off and pickup pattern turns into a fine-tuned machine.

I will admit that the process of dropping off and picking up is cumbersome, and it takes a whole lot longer than one might expect due to the sheer volume of students attending the school. However, after much careful planning and lessons learned, the school has devised the best plan to ensure everyone is safe and the car lines move as efficiently as possible. Every class has a specific drop off/pickup time and route through the school grounds to maximize the flow of traffic for optimal efficiency. So, of course, the school expects that all parents adhere to the plan to ensure the best outcome for everyone. It makes perfect sense that parents would adhere to the "rules" of drop-off and pickup to make everything run smoothly, but alas, there is a percentage that feels their time is so much more valuable than yours. These people watch carefully and try to find some "angle" or way to speed up the process and save themselves that ever so valuable five to ten minutes. Some of these people have invented clever ways to speed up the process and for every clever idea they have, the school eventually finds out and must issue a decree to stop the time saving, rule breaking, and ultimately unsafe idea.

The school is adjacent to a church that has graciously agreed to allow the parents to transit their parking lot during the drop-off and pickup hours. The church made it very clear that parents were not to park in their lot due to the ongoing daily business of the church and the small size of the lot would make it prohibitive for the church to conduct daily business. All parents were told not to use the church parking lot as a drop off or pickup location or a place to park as a shortcut to the traffic line. A certain percentage of parents started ignoring the rule and using the parking lot for their own personal drop-off and pickup location in order to significantly speed up the process. As fate would have it, this began to interfere with the daily business of the church, and they informed the school that this would have to stop or use of the parking lot would end. The school had to send out another decree telling parents that using the church parking lot in ways not in accordance with the agreement would end up restricting our use of the lot altogether and make the entire pickup/drop-off process even worse. Why did the school have to do this?

The "better than the rest of us" brigade was not finished after the church parking lot incident. They were determined to find ways to speed up the process in clear violation of the school rules. The school, realizing they were up against this brigade, took a preemptive strike and put a rule in place to prevent the next incident from occurring. I was pleased that the school recognized what they were dealing with and tried to think ahead of the rule breakers by instituting a "no left turn allowed" out of the school parking lot. The school put up a sign that said no left turn allowed, which made very good sense since the road the parents were exiting onto is a very busy four-lane county highway. The school correctly analyzed and determined that taking a right out of the school parking lot into the flow of traffic would keep the car lane moving quickly, rather than allowing someone to hold up traffic trying to take a left across four lanes of a busy county highway. If you wanted to go left, you first took a right out of the lot and just a few hundred yards down the road was a traffic light that allowed parents to reverse direction if they needed to. Yes, this added a few minutes to the drop-off for those that would have preferred to take a left out of the school parking lot, but it greatly sped up the overall process and shortened everyone's time in the car line. Of course, the "better than the rest of us" brigade determined that this was not convenient and devised yet another clever idea to speed up their process while finding an angle around the "no left turn rule."

The school had clearly decreed that you could not take a left turn and had installed a metal sign saying so; but wait, no one said you could not go straight across!! As fate would have it, the county was building a new road directly across from the school parking lot for access to a new neighborhood. The "better than the rest of us" brigade decided they could dart across the four-lane highway onto the unfinished road, do a U-turn, and then take a right back onto the county highway. This essentially resulted in taking a left onto the very busy highway, although "technically" they were not taking a left out of the lot, but going straight across the road. The end result was the same as if they had been taking a left in the first place since they still had to cut across four lanes of highway traffic. As you can guess, this dramatically slowed down the car line and added time to the entire process for everyone. The school then talked with the county and had them erect roadblocks on the still-under-construction road across the highway to prevent parents from using this tactic. A simple decree telling the parents not to dart across the highway and that "No Left Turn" really meant "No Left Turn" was not enough to stop the "better than the rest of us" brigade. I give the school credit for thinking ahead of this crowd and asking that the road be blocked to keep the rule breakers from continuing to perform this dangerous maneuver despite being asked not to.

This is a very funny and silly example, but all of us witness this kind of behavior on a daily basis. I often think that if we all simply followed the rules for one day, how much better things might work. I am not advocating that we give up our personal freedoms or become robots in a strict autocratic state. Rather, I suggest we try to be respectful and nice to one another by following the rules and working through our civil institutions to change or eliminate the rules we disagree with.

COVID-19 Addendum: The first draft of this chapter was written before the COVID-19 pandemic. I wish I could say that people have gotten better and understand that some rules are in place for the greater good, but that has not been the case. Throughout the country, there have been "mask mandates" and many citizens have either refused to wear masks, or wear them incorrectly, because they claim it infringes on their liberties. Nothing could be further from the truth. The mask mandate is to help slow and limit the spread of COVID-19 so that the most vulnerable among us (older folks and people with co-morbidities, etc.) will not fall ill to the virus and also to avoid overwhelming our medical system. Wearing a "medical grade" mask in an appropriate manner is not exactly my idea of fun, but I do it anyway.

Why do I wear a mask when directed? It was decided by some appointed or elected authority that this small inconvenience would help slow the spread of COVID. I may not agree with a mask mandate or call into question the competence of those issuing the mandate, but I wear it when directed. Those who do not agree with these mandates have recourse through our society, which is built upon the bedrock of the US Constitution and firmly embedded with a respect for the rule of law. Public discourse and disagreement are essential to the survival of our republic, but it must be done in a respectful and civil manner. Simply ignoring a mandate, which has the force of law, might seem like a trivial act, but it begins to create an environment where citizens feel they can ignore or disrespect any law they disagree with. There are certainly times, as articulated by Dr. Martin Luther King in his *Letter from Birmingham Jail*, where he talked about "just and unjust" laws and that peaceful civil disobedience may be warranted when all other measures have failed.

Simply ignoring and disrespecting the rule of law will lead us down a path where we actually have fewer freedoms which could result, worst case, in some form of anarchy. I am a bit concerned by what I see as selfish behavior when fellow citizens decide not to follow a lawful mandate because they think it infringes on their constitutional rights. I wonder how many people complaining about mask mandates have actually read the US Constitution or studied how it has grown and been interpreted by the US Congress and the Supreme Court since its ratification.

The Constitution is a living, breathing document that is ever evolving and improving to protect all our liberties and freedoms. The Constitution is not perfect, nor is the US republic which it created, but the preambular sections states that "In order to form a more perfect union…". The United States is a work in progress and still trying to become a better republic. As Thomas Jefferson was asked by a lady after the Constitutional Convention, "Well Dr. Franklin what have we got a republic or monarchy?"

Franklin responded, "A republic if you can keep it!" (Circa 1787, Constitutional Convention, Philadelphia, PA)

I pray for a future where every US Citizen understands their roles and responsibilities to preserve the freedoms enshrined in the Constitution. This is the only way to keep our republic and guarantee our way of life, which I feel, is among the best in the world.

Some People Are Stupid, but Not YOU, Because:

You understand that we have rules in the United States that exist to preserve order while protecting our freedoms, which serves to promote equality under the law.

Chapter 9
From the Left……

L et me assure you that this is not a political story based on the title, but rather a story of hope, dreams, and vision. In 1970, I was eight years old and attended my first air show at Naval Air Station Quonset Point in North Kingstown, Rhode Island. I can remember every detail of that air show from where we parked, the long walk to the flight line, the static display aircraft, and most importantly, the flight demonstrations. I had never been to an airshow and although I was probably like most eight-year-old boys who thought airplanes were cool, this experience would ignite an incredible love of flying and airplanes that would become my passion. I thought the airplanes, the flight crews and all the displays were very cool and I could not get enough. When the actual flight demonstrations began and I heard the roar of both radial and jet engines, I was hooked for life. The highlight of the show was the performance of the US Navy Blue Angels flight demonstration team. In 1970, the Blue Angels had transitioned to the F-4 Phantom and it was considered the most advanced fighter in its day. As a kid growing up, I had pictures and models of the F-4 Phantom and saw it almost nightly on the evening news due to the US involvement in the Vietnam War. The F4 was the coolest jet in its day and to have an opportunity to see one up close was a thrill!

I remember the pomp and circumstance of the Blue Angels' "preflight" routine, their taxi out and take-off roll. The sound when they selected afterburner was incredible and they seemed to jump into the air and climb away so quicky, only to reappear in a perfectly formed diamond formation!! The show highlighted the performance characteristics of the F-4 Phantom with several maneuvers, formations, inverted flight, and high-speed unrestricted climbs that kept me on the edge of my seat. At the end of the show, the Blue Angels went through their post-flight routine and then approached the crowd to sign autographs and I couldn't wait. The pilots were all so nice and were the perfect recruiters for the US Navy, or in my case, the US Air Force!! None of the pilots left until every kid was the proud owner of a Blue Angels Poster personalized and signed by the entire team and there were A LOT of kids waiting to meet them! They looked like they really enjoyed what they were doing and kept encouraging all of us to pursue our dreams because anything is possible with focus and hard work. I left that air show inspired and determined to pursue my dream of flying the most advanced jets in the world someday.

On the way back to the car, I turned to my father and said, "Someday I am going to fly jets just like the Blue Angels."

I was an excited eight-year-old boy and expected a pat on the head and something along the lines of, "Of course you can do that if you want to."

Instead, my father turned to me and said, "There is no way you will ever be able to do that."

I was shattered to say the least, and could not believe the certainty in his voice that I would never be good enough. I did not live in a positive family environment where a father supports and encourages dreams, but instead shoots them down. Talk about a letdown and a hit to a young ego, I would never tell any of my children they cannot achieve their dreams. In that moment, I suddenly had a spark of clarity that I cannot explain, perhaps it was divine intervention, but from that day forward it was like someone hit a light switch and I decided to rely only on myself and not listen to anyone. I learned to ignore the negative comments and would not let anyone in my family discourage me from pursuing my goals. I stayed focused like a laser beam on my dreams and never let them go. As I look back on this incident, I now feel bad for my father, who probably had his dream stolen from him when he was a boy. I will never know since my father was not around much. He eventually divorced my mother and never had much to do with his children. My father was a sad man and I have spent my whole life trying to be a better man pursuing my dreams and supporting my children as they chase theirs.

Fast forward about sixteen years and I would find myself flying bombers in the US Air Force and, as fate would have it, I was assigned to the Air Show Staff as an additional duty. Additional duties are assigned to every officer in a flying squadron and these duties are on top of a very busy flying, training, and deployment schedule. The Air Show was not considered a glamorous additional duty for a young officer trying to make his/her way in a combat squadron. The airshow "additional duty" was mostly focused on planning and organizing the "open house" on the Air Force base, which consisted of static displays, flying displays, food vendors, and all the nitty gritty of running an air show. What I did not know at the time was that this additional duty would eventually morph into me being involved in Air Force "open house" airshows for about six years and serving as the overall EMCEE and narrator. This additional duty, which I did not want at first, ended up becoming a high-visibility job that would put me in good standing with the base commanders. I became involved in all the aerial flight display scheduling and coordination, and narrated for many of the aerial performances. The air show would typically feature the Air Force Thunderbirds flight demonstration team and I would introduce them before their narrator took over for their demonstration.

On a typical airshow weekend while I was stationed at McConnel AFB in Kansas, we hosted well over two hundred thousand visitors and I became very comfortable talking to crowds of over one hundred thousand on both the Saturday and Sunday shows. It was a thrill to be involved in air shows and as I gained experience and credibility, I also was added to the flight demonstration team for the B-1B Bomber. I was living my dream a couple weekends a month flying and performing for crowds throughout the United States and Canada. Most Air Force squadrons have dedicated crews that are "checked out" on the air show maneuvers which have been approved by headquarters and this is a great opportunity to showcase the capabilities of all the jets in the Air Force inventory. In this capacity, myself and a few other crews would alternate attending and performing in air shows. For some of the larger air shows, we would fly in with two B-1Bs and on the first day, one crew would fly and the other would stand in front of the second B-1B to do a "static display." The crew not flying would answer questions, sign autographs, and also narrate the flight demonstration while their wingman performed. I am not certain what a rock star feels like when they perform in front of thousands of fans, but in many ways, I felt like a rock star, although not as well compensated!!

I enjoyed the flying aspect of the demonstration and often we would be piped in "live" from the cockpit over the PA system to talk to the audience while performing the maneuvers. It was a big thrill to actually talk to the crowd while we were performing the aerial maneuvers and it gave them a sense of what it is like to fly the most advanced bomber in the world.

"Pilot," I would say, "turn to heading 090 degrees and accelerate to 600 knots for the bomb run."

"Roger that," the pilot would reply, "turning and accelerating for the bomb run."

"Stand by for the weapons delivery checklist," I continued. "Target acquired, weapons selected, final aiming looks good."

"Weapons doors opening, stand by, 3-2-1 weapons away," I

would broadcast over the live PA system.

At this point we usually had "flash pots" set up near the runway that were ignited as we passed. These flash pots simulated a small weapons detonation along with loud bangs, flames, and plenty of smoke. The flash pots were a crowd pleaser and the crowd often erupted into cheers and applause.

"Post release checklist complete, start your climb," I added.

We would keep the wings swept aft and start a near vertical climb at over 600 knots to simulate egressing from an enemy target area. We felt pretty cool, but we could not see or hear the crowd since we were focused on the task at hand. But we assumed the crowd was loving it.

Narrating was also a lot of fun since you could actually see the crowd right in front of you and their reactions while your wingman was putting the jet through its paces. One of the maneuvers we performed was a high-speed pass with the wings in the fully swept aft position. If you have never seen a B-1B do a high-speed pass at about one hundred feet above the runway, I can tell you it is very impressive. The maneuver was flown at .99 Mach, just under the sound barrier, which created a quiet and beautiful pass. I would announce to the crowd in my best air show narrator voice, "Ladies and gentleman, from the left, your United States Air Force B-1B Bomber!"

As the crowd turned their heads to the left, they could see the B-1B approaching the airfield at over 600 knots or about 700 miles per hour.

The interesting thing that most people do not anticipate is when you fly just below the sound barrier, the actual jet noise is about one to two seconds "behind" the jet, so as the jet approaches, it is absolutely quiet. Slowly you begin to hear the sound catch up, but it is the distant sound of the jet since it is lagging and when the jet crosses show center it is eerily quiet and very beautiful. The tranquility fades away as the noise catches up with the jet and soon thereafter comes the noise of four afterburner jet engines producing 120,000 pounds of thrust!! It catches many by surprise since they are looking the other direction watching the B-1B pull away into a near vertical climb and set up for the next maneuverer. Watching the faces of the crowd as the noise approaches is priceless since it is VERY LOUD and catches most of them off guard. The jet noise is so loud it shakes everything within several hundred yards of the flight line and typically sets off every car alarm in the parking lot!! As the noise reaches its peak and then starts to taper off, you are left with the noise of hundreds of car alarms and only then can it be considered a successful flyby! The rest of the show demonstrated the flight characteristics of the B-1B and it was always a crowd favorite to see such a large plane maneuvering and performing like a fighter jet on steroids.

After the show, we would be swarmed by the crowd and, just like the Blue Angels pilots had done for me when I was eight years old, I stayed until every last person had a chance to meet with us. I signed every program, picture, and poster, and posed for hundreds of photos. I always thought every time I got to do this how lucky I was to be able to give back. When asked by the kids if they could fly B-1Bs someday, I always said, "Of course you can and do not let anyone tell you otherwise. Work hard and stay focused on your dreams and anything is possible!"

<u>Some People Are Stupid, but Not YOU, Because:</u>

You understand that when we realize our dreams,
it is expected we give back and pay it forward.

Chapter 10
I Love My Children

The title of this chapter suggests I am going to write about the love I have for my children. However, that is not the focus of this story. Of course I love my children, but this story is about a woman who loves her children very much and whom I have never met. In fact, I really do not know what this woman looks like, where she lives, what she does, or anything else for that matter, but I do know that she loves her children.

I was driving home from the office one evening and was caught in typical rush hour traffic as I replayed the events of the day and listened to the radio. I use my commute home as a sort of unwinding from the stress of the day, so when I get home I am not still consumed with work. I tend not to bring my work home and learned a long time ago that not shutting down the office in your brain is unhealthy over a long period of time. There are jobs and times that demand we be "on our game" nearly every hour of the day, but if you are fortunate not to have to be switched on all the time, then take the chance to unwind. My drive helps me do this and I am always looking for ways to shift my focus from the office to home.

The traffic was moving pretty good for the time of day and we were nearly at highway speeds moving along like a line of racecars drafting each other's bumpers. At these relatively close distances and slower speeds, I tend to have more time to catch up on my reading, bumper sticker reading that is! I personally do not have bumper stickers on my car for no other reason than I simply do not want anything stuck to my car that announces something about me to a bunch of total strangers. Who really cares if "I Would Rather Be Fishing," or my student is on the honor role, or who I voted for in the last election? I certainly do not really care to know this about other people. However, despite my reluctance to put bumper stickers on my car, I really do appreciate them and think that many of them are rather clever and make me laugh while cruising down the highway. In addition, bumper stickers represent the true expression of free speech and Second Amendment rights, so I say keep adding them to your bumpers if you are so inclined. I also believe that if you have a sticker on your bumper, you are telling the world something about yourself by virtue of having affixed the sticker to your bumper, and you have consented to share this information.

When I see a bumper sticker that is very amusing, politically stimulating, very touching, or anything else, I begin to create a mental image of what the person driving the car must be like. For example, if I see a bumper sticker that says, "I Would Rather Be Fishing," I begin to create an image of a person that likes to be outdoors near or on the water, who enjoys the challenge of trying to catch the elusive Big Fish, and I bet has all the gear to make this happen. This person is probably someone that really enjoys the water and hanging out for long periods of time contemplating life with the sporadic adrenaline rush when the bait is taken. I think I would enjoy hanging out with this sort of person, not because I like fishing, but because I like beer and I have never been on a fishing trip that did not involve beer. So there you have it, bumper stickers help me unwind during my commute and form some funny impressions of my fellow commuters.

I slowly closed the distance between a minivan and myself during my commute and as fate would have it, there was a very touching bumper sticker affixed to the back of the vehicle. This bumper sticker warmed my heart, and it simply said, "I Love My Children" in big bold letters. I began to form my mental image of the person driving this minivan and I could tell from the shadow cast on the tinted back window that a woman was behind the wheel based on the silhouette and hairstyle. I immediately began to think what a wonderful person and mother she is because rather than assuming people would understand how devoted she was to her children (as we all are), she wanted to step up her game a bit and announce it to the whole world, or at least those of us that ever drove behind her! My image of this woman so devoted to her children made me glow with admiration and respect for being brave enough to announce this to everyone. She must really be the "super mom" that goes the extra distance to ensure her children are raised in a loving, safe, and respectful environment. Her children must be wonderful kids and on the path to being very nice adults and future contributing citizens in our communities. I am not brave enough to declare this publicly on my bumper, even though I do love my children more than anything. I am far too human and there are days I would prefer not to announce my love for my children when they have pushed every button to drive me crazy. I wanted to meet this "super mom" and if I were lucky, maybe she would share a parenting tip or two. I thought I was riding behind a real saint, the Mother of Mother Teresa perhaps! She must be so good under fire and so understanding and loving that nothing gets in the way of "super mom."

Suddenly, the traffic began to move along a bit faster and I had the opportunity to shift into the left lane and slowly begin to pass the minivan. I was eager to catch a glimpse of the woman, I mean Saint, that was at the wheel so I could see what a "super mom" looked like. As I began to pass the minivan, I could see into the side windows and very discreetly started looking to my right so I could catch a glimpse. The side windows were not tinted, so I had a very clear view into the minivan. And there I saw three children riding in the back of the minivan, and I thought how lucky they were to have "super mom." As I came alongside the minivan, I saw something very alarming. There in the back seats of this minivan cruising along at 65 MPH were "super mom's" three children bouncing around, climbing over seats, and messing around without a care in the world for their safety. How could this be? I was shocked that this saint of a "super mom" would let her children ride in a vehicle without their seatbelts on!! Didn't she know how dangerous that is? Didn't she just announce to the world how much she loves her children?

I was very disappointed, but I thought that even "super moms" have bad days and I was willing to look the other way until I got alongside "super mom" herself. There she was driving down the highway with all three of her kids not wearing seatbelts in bumper-to-bumper traffic that often stops on a dime for no reason. But to make matters worse, she had her cell phone up to her ear which can easily cause distracted driving. Of course, the seatbelts would be enough to take away her "super mom" title, and I can forgive the cellphone since we do not have a hands-free law in Colorado, but in addition, she was smoking a cigarette with all the windows rolled up. Did she not realize that secondhand smoke in a confined space like a minivan is bad for her children? How could she say she loves her children and proclaim this to all of us when clearly, she did not take their safety very seriously? I decided that she was not "super mom" and was human like the rest of us and not deserving of her bumper sticker, but this is a free country.

Some People Are Stupid, but Not YOU, Because:

You realize that parenting and loving our children often involves making decisions and doing things that are not popular so our children have the opportunity to grow up in a safe environment.

Chapter 11
Screw Communism

I n late 1985, I was on my way to flight school during the height of the Cold War. Ronald Reagan was President and Commander in Chief enjoying his second term in the Oval Office. It had long been a stated goal of President Reagan to end the Cold War and bring the Soviet Union (USSR–Union of Soviet Socialist Republics) to its knees. Reagan's plan was quite simple: engage the Soviet Union in an arms race that its weak state-run economy could not sustain. In a speech Reagan gave in 1983, he referred to the Soviet Union as *"The Evil Empire"* and pointed out that, *"as good Marxist-Leninists, the Soviet Leaders have openly and publicly declared that the only morality they recognize is that which will further their cause, which is world revolution."* (March 8, 1983 address to the National Association of Evangelicals in Orlando, Florida.)

The USSR was front and center during Reagan's presidency and he understood that totalitarian regimes were wrong. Russian citizens were being oppressed with little freedom or ability to pursue their own version of happiness. Regan characterized the battle between America and the USSR as a battle between Good and Evil. This was the environment under which I went to flight school and it seemed so obvious that the Soviet Union was flawed and that their system of government was not working, except for those in positions of power and authority. In a very real way, it was nice to have "The Evil Empire" to focus on as our principal and most dangerous enemy, and a Commander in Chief with the courage to say so.

The Cold War was a state of political and military tension that began after World War II between the Eastern Bloc (predominately the USSR and her allies) and the United States (predominately the US and her allies) that lasted from approximately 1947 to 1991. During the forty-four years of the Cold War, both sides were focused on expanding their spheres of influence and promoting their version of political ideology by demonizing the other side's ideology. The primary difference was that the USSR and her allies were promoting a communist ideology that "looked great on paper," but in actual practice was authoritarian, with little respect for human rights.

Meanwhile, the United States and her allies were promoting a Republican and Democratic system of governance that certainly had its flaws, but the focus was on individual rights, freedoms, and the ability to create a good quality of life if you worked hard. During the period between 1947 and 1982, it has been conservatively estimated that approximately nine million people emigrated to the West from the Eastern Bloc states of Albania, Bulgaria, Czechoslovakia, East Germany, Hungary, Poland, Romania, and the Soviet Union.

If Communism was so wonderful, then why were so many people leaving these countries and coming to the West? Those of us in the military studied the intelligence almost daily, which clearly showed that life under Communist rule for the vast majority of citizens was miserable. The Russian Communist Party was trying to create a society based on the utopian ideal of equality and abundance, as expressed by the popular slogan, "From each according to his ability, to each according to his need."

Communism in practice has only ever existed under authoritarian governments and has been the source of millions of human rights violations and deaths. The Eastern Bloc, lead by the USSR, was trying to expand their influence around the globe, and Cold War Warriors like myself were not going to allow that to happen.

In the Fall of 1986, I was assigned to Loring Air Force Base in Northern Maine, known as a "Northern Tier" assignment because of its proximity to the Polar Circle and the USSR. I had just completed my B-52 training and was eager to report to my first bomb squadron and start my qualification process to become combat qualified so I could sit alert. The process of qualification took an additional six months before I was declared fully combat qualified and I began sitting alert with an armed bomber for seven days at a time every third week. From 1986 until the Cold War officially ended in 1991, I had logged well over sixty weeks of alert duty and was proud to say I did my part to deter the USSR from ever launching a nuclear attack against the United States. During this time, the doctrine, Mutually Assured Destruction (MAD), sent a clear message to the USSR that the United States would retaliate against any nuclear attack with an overwhelming response. And to prove we were serious, the Nuclear Triad of Manned Bombers, Missiles, and Submarines were on constant ready alert 365 days a year around the clock.

Most Americans probably did not think about this constant state of alert and our posture to deter any Soviet aggression, but I was happy to be the silent warrior protecting Americans while they went about their daily lives enjoying all of the freedoms that this alert posture guaranteed. I knew then that the Cold War and the arms race were unsustainable for the USSR and eventually they would collapse under the weight of an arms race that their economy could not support. The Soviet Collapse began in 1986 under Gorbochev and his era of "Glasnost," or openness, which initially was an attempt to "boost" the Communist system and global expansion while trying to open up the Soviets to more cooperative international and economic agreements. Those of us that studied the USSR knew that this was the beginning of the end, and eventually the Soviets would begin to curb their global revolutionary ambitions and stop pointing a loaded gun at the United States and her allies.

I studied my enemy very closely and really began to feel strong animus towards Communist ideology, which looked great in theory, but in practice was a lie, and innocent civilians were suffering. The only people doing well in the Communist states were those in power, and that remains the case to this very day. Today, in the two largest Communist powers, the Former Soviet Union and China, repression and human rights abuses are rampant and go unchecked. Recently, in April 2016, it was revealed that at least three of the seven people on the Chinese Communist Party's most powerful committee, including President Xi Jinping, have relatives who have controlled secretive offshore companies. *(According to leaked documents known as the "Panama Papers—Leaked from "Mossack Fonseca Law Firm"—A boutique law firm in Panama that specializes in creating tax shelters and secretive corporations for wealthy clients.)*

In addition, Cellist Sergei Roldugin, a close friend of President Vladimir V. Putin of Russia, was also named in the Panama documents. Mr. Roldugin is at the center of a $2 billion scheme "in which money from Russian state banks is hidden offshore." The average Russian and Chinese citizen has absolutely no recourse from stopping these types of abuses due to personal greed. The very nature of humans (ambition, greed, etc.) is removed from Communist ideology as the perfect society is created, however, in reality human nature cannot be tamed in any system of governance. Human nature can only be controlled and dealt with in a form of government that has a strong judicial system founded on respect for the rule of law and the protection of personal rights and freedoms. I hate Communism.

As mentioned earlier, I reported into my first B-52 Bomb Squadron in the fall of 1986, eager to start my squadron qualification process. I had just spent the previous six months learning all the B-52 weapons systems and combat tactics. As a young lieutenant, my first course of action was to report into the squadron so I could end my leave and "formally" be attached to the squadron. It was a Friday afternoon and I walked into the 69th Bomb Squadron orderly room to officially sign in and meet the commander. When I walked into the squadron, it was a ghost town and no one could be found. I was surprised at first and then found a wonderful staff sergeant who was in charge of the orderly room and signed me in as the newest member of the "Fighting 69th."

I asked the sergeant, "Where is everyone?"

He replied, "Well sir, they have all departed a bit early today for a special celebration at the Officer's Club."

The sergeant continued, "I recommend you head over to the club, sir, to meet the commander and the other officers."

"OK," I said. "Not a bad way to start my first assignment at a social event!"

The Sergeant did not give me much more information, but pointed in the direction of the Officer's Club, and I dutifully obeyed his advice and headed straight there.

I figured it must be some kind of promotion or celebration of great significance, since the entire squadron was in attendance at the club. I arrived at the Officer's Club to find my entire squadron having a wonderful celebration and I immediately joined in and set out to find my new commander. As I walked in, several of my new squadron mates greeted me as I introduced myself and I was immediately welcomed to the squadron. I met several of the senior staff and most everyone else, but had not met the commander yet and was eager simply to say hello and let him know I was there. Before I could find the commander, I asked what the occasion was for the great celebration and a senior officer in the squadron explained to me that this was the Bomb Squadron's celebration of the anniversary of the publication of the Communist Manifesto by Karl Marx. At first, I was taken aback. "Why the hell would we celebrate the publication of the Communist Manifesto?"

I was directed towards the back of the club to meet the commander and the sight that awaited me would explain everything. As I arrived at the back of the club, it opened up to a patio area and a large lawn of nice green grass and a crowd of officers laughing and yelling at something I could not yet see. I pushed through the crowd and repeatedly asked, "Where is the commander?" I was told he was out on the lawn, and as I made my way to the front to introduce myself, I saw the most incredible thing. On the beautiful green lawn was a perfectly chalked outline of the entire USSR that covered at least fifteen yards of grass and was very accurate. Standing inside the chalked area was a lieutenant colonel who I would learn later was my commander, swinging a fishing pole with a Russian bear bomber attached to one end. My commander was swinging this bear bomber across the entire outline of the USSR and the Russian bear had been lit on fire. It was a magnificent sight to see this model airplane burning while being swung back and forth across the USSR, and the contrast with the green grass was striking. All of the officers were chanting in unison, "Screw Communism!" and it was at this point I noticed the large banner across the back of the Officer's Club. *(Author's Note: It was a bit more of a colorful party title starting with an F-word, but I decided to keep that out of the story!)*

This was a "Screw Communism" party on the anniversary of the publication of the Communist Manifesto. I immediately felt right at home and I eventually met my commander who welcomed me and told me to "grab a beer."

We all toasted and declared our freedom from Communism. A very fitting arrival for a young lieutenant to his first squadron, and I was now among brothers. I hate Communism.

Some People Are Stupid, but Not YOU, Because:

You know that freedom and a good quality of life only come through hard work, sacrifice, and a system of government based on respect for the rule of law which protects civil liberties and rights, while also creating an environment for free market competition.

<u>A Caution Regarding the Welfare State</u>

"You cannot legislate the poor into freedom by legislating the wealthy out of freedom. What one person receives without working for, another person must work for without receiving. The government cannot give to anybody anything that the government does not first take from somebody else. When half of the people get the idea that they do not have to work because the other half is going to take care of them, and when the other half gets the idea that it does no good to work because somebody else is going to get what they work for, that my dear friend, is about the end of any nation. You cannot multiply wealth by dividing it."

~~~~~ Dr. Adrian Rogers, 1931 - 2005 ~~~~~

Chapter 12
Rolling the Bone—
Character and Integrity

The two most important things we possess are Character and Integrity. Throughout my career and growing up, your word was your bond and breaking it was a direct assault on your character and integrity. I try to avoid conflict and find solutions to most problems that life throws my way, but when there is a question of my character or integrity, the gloves come off. We have little control over what happens to us in life and can only prepare the best we can for all of the challenges ahead. I would submit that if you do not have a strong personal foundation built on strength of character, then the challenges will appear much worse and harder to cope with. Anyone can lead and make good decisions when things are going along in a steady and predictable manner. But when the storm hits, true leaders emerge and make good decisions based on their strength of character and impeccable integrity. When everyone is watching, doing the right thing is wonderful, but when no one is watching, doing the right thing is greatness.

While serving as a commissioned officer in the US Air Force, I was expected to be a man of my word and do the right thing when no one else was watching. I can say that I made many mistakes and poor decisions along the way, but always tried to do the right thing according to the information and facts I had on hand. I, along with three crewmembers, were entrusted with a $300 million aircraft, and we were expected to become experts at its employment in the most challenging environment. Flying at 600 knots (about 690 miles per hour), at 400 feet at night, in the weather through mountains in Automatic Terrain Following Mode is not a good time to find out you have weak character and questionable integrity. I trusted everyone on my crew with my life and I expected them to make good decisions based on the information and situation we were facing. We had to rely on one another, and this story is told over and over again throughout the aviation world from WWII to present day. Each member of the B-1B crew has a critical role to perform and your crew is depending on you to do it well. I never questioned my fellow officers and crewmembers and trusted them with my life; however, one day along came a man of questionable integrity.

I was assigned to the 28th Bomb Squadron (BS) in Wichita, KS, flying the B-1B Bomber and loving every minute of it. I was a young Offensive Systems Officer (OSO) and was the newest addition to the squadron. Initially, when arriving as a new aviator to the 28th BS, you are assigned to training flight to complete your local procedures and weapons qualifications before being declared a combat mission capable crewmember. I had been flying non-stop in training flight with several different flight instructors as I got checked out on everything from air refueling radar rendezvous, to low level automatic terrain following, target ID and weapons delivery, management of all the onboard computers, and emergency procedures, just to name a few. The checkout process took about five to six months and I was almost done with my checkout and only needed one more live weapons drop to complete the program. I was assigned to fly with an instructor pilot and instructor OSO from training flight, and a regular squadron pilot who was completing his final flight in the B-1B. The second pilot was separating from the Air Force within a few days to pursue a career flying with the airlines. In the Air Force, it is tradition to have a "Fini Flight" or final sortie in your weapon system as a farewell before you transition to another assignment, or into civilian life. We planned a sortie out to the Utah Test and Training Range to complete a live weapons release for a Friday, taking off in the morning and returning late in the afternoon.

The B-1B was quite a remarkable jet to fly, and it had so much more capability than any other bomber at the time. The jet also had incredible speed, could exceed the sound barrier while cruising along at four hundred feet, and was highly maneuverable. We also felt that if we ran into enemy defenses, we would have speed, maneuverability, and electronic countermeasures that would make the jet very survivable. No fighter in the world could catch us going that fast at four hundred feet before running out of fuel. In order for a fighter to catch us, they had to burn extraordinary amounts of fuel in afterburner, which is a luxury fighters do not have. The B-1B carried so much fuel that we had enough capacity for forty-five minutes of afterburner (although you would never stay in that long for many reasons) while most fighters have minutes, if not seconds, in afterburner to attain high speeds.

The reason for the discussion about the maneuverability of the B-1B is simply to highlight that we found ourselves flying an incredible airframe built by Rockwell that opened up the tactical possibilities of a low-level penetrating bomber. It had become an unofficial tradition after a very good weapons delivery during our post target climb to do a "victory roll," or what is known as an aileron roll. This maneuver was not prohibited, and it was well within the capabilities of the jet; it was also not specifically authorized, so the maneuver clearly fell into the gray area. I first experienced this maneuver while I was in the B-1B training program at Dyess AFB, Texas, after having completed my final check flight. No one really talked about this maneuver, although we heard about it in the squadron and it was performed from time to time after a successful mission. Anyone who flies airplanes knows that an aileron roll, if done correctly, is a 1-G maneuver and places no additional stress on the airframe. The maneuver was not prohibited, so crews did it from time to time, and it was fairly well known among the B-1B crews and commanders that this was occurring, but again, one really talked about.

Of course, all good things must eventually come to an end. My final training flight out to the Utah Test Range had been going well and we were approaching our target run.

"Pilot," I said, "turn right to 268 degrees for the initial point and accelerate to 600 knots."

The initial point was the beginning of the bomb run and I was very busy running the bomb run checklist. The instructor tried to make it realistic and called out several enemy threats that required us to take evasive action to avoid simulated surface-to-air missiles and flak. This made acquiring the target much more difficult, but in between maneuvers, I took a radar snapshot of the target and had us well lined up. The B-1B had an incredible radar system and would freeze an image so the OSO could refine aiming while the jet maneuvered during our ingress.

I chimed in, "Pilot, OSO, the heading mark and speed bar are good and the target aim point is acquired. Ten seconds to release."

"Roger that," replied the pilot. "Autopilot coupled."

We always released weapons in "full coupled" mode since the computers, along with my aim points adjustments, were constantly calculating and updating the ballistics and desired release point. The onboard computers were, and still are, much quicker adjusting the release point and flying the jet than any crewmember could ever hope to be.

"Ten, nine, eight," I counted, "bay doors opening, three, two, one, weapons away, cleared to maneuver!"

We could feel the slight "bump" as the two thousand-pound weapon departed the jet and the pilot immediately went into a 60-degree post target egress turn to avoid simulated enemy ground fire.

We had flown into the target area and released our weapon exactly on time (the tolerance was plus or minus three seconds) and we "shacked" or had a direct hit on the target. After the initial egress turn, we returned to straight and level flight, leveled off, and started a climb to exit the weapons range. We were all very pleased with the weapons delivery and were busy running the post-release checklist and climb checklist to exit the range. The co-pilot, the guy on his final B-1B flight, did a perfect aileron roll as we exited the range and leveled off exactly at our assigned altitude. The rest of the sortie was uneventful, and we arrived back at our base in Kansas late on a Friday afternoon.

After every sortie, the crew gets together to complete a bunch of post flight paperwork and, most importantly, to have a thorough debriefing to gather lessons learned from the sortie. My instructor was pleased with my performance and had a few suggestions to help me improve my technique, but at the end of the day, I was signed off and would become a combat mission capable crewmember. I was pleased to have completed this phase of my training and already knew which crew I would be assigned to. I was very excited to be a "regular guy" around the squadron.

As we continued our debriefing, the operations officer, the second in command in an AF squadron, came into our debriefing room and said to my instructor, "We need you to fly another sortie Monday morning. So when you are done here, we need you down the hall to mission plan with another crew, please."

"Yes sir," my instructor replied. "Just a few more minutes and I will be right there."

The operations officer also reported that the squadron held a commander's call earlier in the afternoon. The commander's call is a fairly standard Friday meeting, when the whole squadron gathers to review events of the past week, preview the upcoming week, and generally enjoy squadron camaraderie. We were flying while this meeting was being held, so the operations officer needed to tell us about a new policy just instituted by the commander.

The operations officer then said, "I know we have been a bit lax on the rolling after target maneuver, but the commander has decided to officially ban the post target rolling maneuver."

The operations officer continued, "In recent weeks, we have had too many over Gs and that could shorten the service life of the jet."

All good things come to an end and we knew that sooner or later this maneuver would be banned. We acknowledged the new policy and committed not to do it anymore. We also understood that if a jet was rolled, it was our duty to report the incident. We had no problem with the new policy and knew it was in the best interest of extending the service life of the B-1B.

But, we were presented with a conundrum regarding the no rolling policy. During the time the commander was informing the squadron about the policy, we were thousands of miles away operating under the old "non-policy" and performed a post target aileron roll. Should we report this incident to the commander?

The instructor pilot then said, "OK guys, you heard the operations officer. How do you want to handle this?"

The co-pilot said, "Since the policy was put in place while we were flying, I think it is best just to salute smartly and ensure going forward it never happens again."

I added, "I think since we were not aware of the policy at the time, we are probably ok not to report this incident, but moving forward we should never roll the jet again and report anyone who does."

The others in the room agreed with my logic, but the pilot asked again, "OK, do we agree to keep this incident to ourselves or go tell the commander?"

All four crewmembers nodded their heads in agreement and the pilot said, "OK, if there is anything further or anyone has a change of heart, we will go see the commander."

We all nodded our heads in agreement and felt that since the policy was instituted while we were flying, there was no reason to report it. Perhaps it was not the best decision to not to report the rolling incident, but we gave each other our word and moved on. My instructor completed his paperwork and left the three of us so he could start mission planning for the following Monday mission. The rest of us took about another hour to complete our paperwork and debriefing. It was late on a Friday afternoon, so once everything was completed, we started to head home to enjoy the weekend.

I was walking to my car and I heard a yell from the squadron. It was my instructor pilot. "Jim, come back. The commander wants to see us."

I turned to see my instructor pilot standing in the door and wondered what the squadron commander wanted to see us about. I approached the door and asked, "Do you know why the commander wants to see us?"

My pilot replied that the instructor OSO had a change of mind and reported all of us to the commander for having rolled the jet earlier in the day. I could not believe my ears and was completely shocked. "Are you kidding me? We decided it was not relevant to report today's incident as a crew."

I had never in my life been so hung out to dry and was floored that someone whom I trusted and respected had gone back on his word. At least he could have come back into our briefing room and said, "You know guys, I am not feeling good about this decision," at which point we would have walked into the commander's office as a crew to report the incident.

Please understand that this individual was still in the squadron and in the next room from ours. I had walked past his mission planning room several times as we were completing our paperwork, and there had been plenty of opportunity for him to call us back together. It would have been the right thing to do. Instead, this individual walked right past our open door and into the commander's office and hung us out. I have never had an issue with the instructor OSO's change of heart, but rather the way he did it. We were not given the chance to revisit the issue and go into the commander's office as a crew. The issue with the commander now was not that we had rolled the jet; he did not care; now the issue was about our integrity since we decided to keep it from him.

The meeting with the commander was not very pleasant, to say the least. We entered the commander's office, came to attention, and the instructor pilot saluted and said, "Reporting as ordered, sir."

The commander then said, "I think all of you know why I have called you in here?" He continued, "It has been brought to my attention that you rolled the jet post target and that you had decided to not report the incident. I understand the policy was put in place while you were flying, but this maneuver is now banned and must be reported in every case. Do all of you understand that?"

Collectively we all said, "Yes sir, we understand."

The commander then said, "I am more concerned about the decision not to report this event and I am unsure of what action I will take next. You are all ordered to be available over the weekend as I work through the issue and next steps, including possible disciplinary actions."

This was an uncomfortable position and the commander then asked if we had anything to say.

The co-pilot chimed in, "Sir, it is totally my fault. I was flying the jet and performed the roll without any prior coordination or announcing it to the crew."

In an effort to defend the instructor pilot, I then said, "Sir, I realize the major issue is the decision not to report it, but if it matters at all, I can attest to the fact that the roll was a perfect 1-G maneuver."

This attempt to help the instructor pilot seemed to fall on deaf ears, so I added, "Sir, it was such a smooth maneuver you could hardly tell the jet had been rolled."

My statement was aimed at helping the instructor pilot who I knew was going to bear the brunt of any disciplinary action. The instructor OSO either did not hear clearly what I said, or decided to ignore it, and would go on to report to others in the squadron that I had lost my "situational awareness" and falsely said I did not know the jet had been rolled. Losing one's situational awareness while flying an Air Force high performance jet is a very serious issue and can lead to a loss of flight status. This statement was a lie, and the instructor OSO spread this through the squadron despite my efforts to report what I actually had said. The damage was done and insult was added to injury.

During the weekend, we received a phone call that we were to report to the commander's office first thing on Monday morning. The instructor OSO was completely exonerated and the instructor pilot and I received formal letters of reprimand. The co-pilot was allowed to separate from the Air Force as planned with no negative comments on his flight records and went on to have a successful career with the airlines. I was young enough in the squadron and still several years away from my next promotion, so I had plenty of time to overcome this incident. I worked hard over the next few years to successfully restore my good name, character, and integrity. Luckily, my Air Force career was not impacted negatively by this incident and I would go on to make colonel.

The instructor pilot, who was already a major, was not so lucky, and took the brunt of the punishment. He would go onto what I think was a less than desirable next assignment and was ultimately passed over for promotion. Of course, I cannot say that this incident is the reason the instructor pilot was passed over for further promotion, but I can say with all certainty it did not help. The instructor OSO left the squadron for another assignment within months of the episode and would go on to have a long Air Force career. I have no hard feelings or anger towards this individual, but I certainly endeavored the rest of my long Air Force career to ensure our paths never crossed again.

The point of the story is simply to highlight that we must be the kind of people that honor their word with the strongest of character and the utmost integrity. If you find yourself in a situation where you must go back on your word due to some change of heart, new information, or whatever, do it in the light of day.

Some People Are Stupid, but Not YOU, Because:

You understand that Strong Character and Integrity are the most important things in our lives, and when you give your word, you stand by it!

Chapter 13
Lightning Strikes Twice

On a daily basis, I am reminded how lucky I am to have so many blessings in my life. As of this writing, I have been happily married to the same woman for over thirty years, have four wonderful children that are maturing into fine young adults and good citizens, and we have our health. In addition, we have enough resources to live our lives the way we choose in this great country, and although we are far from wealthy, we have what we need to make ends meet. If I said I have never taken any of this for granted, I would be lying. During my career, I have always focused on the next step or promotion and worked hard to get there, often forgetting to smell the roses along the way. Sometimes we all get caught up in the daily grind of life and forget to count our blessings and enjoy the view during the climb. Fortunately, during two separate instances in my life, I was given a reminder to slow down once in a while and enjoy the scenery.

In 1993, I was stationed at McConnell AFB in Wichita, Kansas, flying B-1B Bombers. I was a senior captain and things were going well in my squadron. I had recently earned my instructor and evaluator rating, which is very important for an Air Force flying career and being competitive for the next promotion. I was involved in almost every additional duty or special project my squadron had going on, and I was trying to distinguish myself from about a hundred other officers in my squadron that were also Type As and aviation superheroes! All the officers in a combat flying squadron are very competitive and everyone burns the candle at both ends to "stand out" among the greatest aviators on earth (or so we were told), and somehow get one of the few promotion slots. In the middle of this culture, I was not interested in the roses or the view along the way and can honestly say I was not counting my blessings as much as I should have been.

I was flying a fairly typical nighttime B-1B mission involving formation work, air refueling, and a low level with a scheduled weapon delivery. The mission was going fine, and it was a hot Kansas evening with a forecast for mostly clear skies and the chance of a thunderstorm. My wingman entered the low level route ahead of us and dropped down to five hundred feet on automatic terrain following and 550 knots. I entered about one minute behind him, which gave us about nine miles separation on the route, and everything was working fine. The night was dark but clear, and we could see the stars above and the ground below. The jet was performing as designed. We were hitting all of our low-level checkpoints within plus or minus three seconds of our scheduled times and the weapon pre-arming and preparation went smoothly. Up ahead, our wingman entered the bomb run and radioed back to us, "Two, lead here."

We replied, "Two here, go ahead lead."

Our wingman then said, "Just FYI, we are tracking a thunderstorm located about ten to fifteen miles due east of the bomb run initial point and we are seeing lightning."

"Roger that lead," we replied. "We will keep an eye on it."

Anyone who has ever flown an airplane knows that thunderstorms and airplanes do not mix very well and we take thunderstorms VERY seriously. I looked at the route and noted the thunderstorm's location. It appeared to be well outside of our planned route, so we decided to continue with the mission.

As we approached the initial point for the bomb run, we could see the storm well off to the right of the route. On the radar, I determined that it was about ten to twelve miles away. Based on the distance, and in accordance with AF regulations, we needed to maintain a ten-mile distance when operating at or below ten thousand feet. I informed the pilot, "According to the radar, we have ten miles separation and are cleared to proceed."

"Roger that," the pilot replied. "We are turning inbound to the bomb run heading and accelerating."

As we turned inbound, I began running through our weapons release checklist while also acquiring the target and offset aim points on the radar. The run was looking good until all of a sudden and without warning there was a HUGE EXPLOSION and a sudden blinding flash of light. We had been hit by lightning and were so busy with the bomb run that it really caught all of us by surprise, and I was struck in the foot and lost consciousness for a few seconds. Although we were ten miles away from the storm and well within our safety protocols, it is a known fact that thunderstorms can still "throw" lightning anywhere from ten to twenty miles downrange. There is a strange phenomenon in the lightning world known as ball lightning and it is literally a "ball of lightning" that forms when a bolt strikes and discharges electricity. In this instance, the strike hit the nose of the aircraft and a ball of lightning emerged from the center of the cockpit console, hitting me in the foot! My crewmember at the time reported that he saw this ball of electricity fly through the cockpit and "explode" on my foot.

I only saw the bright light and felt the explosion on my foot; the rest gets a bit fuzzy. I lost consciousness for a few seconds, and when I came to, I could see that the entire cockpit was black and without electricity. As background, the B-1B is an electric jet and the bold face for complete electrical failure is "Ejection Handle Pull"! As I was regaining consciousness, my hands were reaching for the ejection handle since I thought the jet had lost all electricity. In the faint distance, I heard my crewmember say, "Jim, it is OK. Stay with us!"

When I heard my crewmember, I overrode my trained instinct to eject and took my hands off the ejection handles. As I regained consciousness, I realized that the lightning strike had disrupted the terrain following system which put us into an automatic fly-up away from the ground, a safety feature built into the B-1B Terrain Following System that probably saved all our lives that night.

After a few seconds, which seemed forever, the jet came back to life and all systems and computers came back online. Of course, not really knowing to what extent the jet might have been damaged, and given my loss of consciousness, we declared an emergency and returned to base. As we flew back to base, I started to realize what had just happened and that I had survived being hit by lightning. I was thankful for the rubber-soled boots I was wearing and that I had not taken the full brunt of the lightning bolt. When we landed, I was escorted to the hospital where they did a full examination along with an EKG to ensure my heart was working OK. Everything seemed fine and I was released from the hospital later that night having been given the all clear from the medical staff. Despite some numbness for a few days, I had no untoward effects and was back on the flight schedule within days, although I did try to slow down a bit and count my blessings.

Fast-forward several years to the summer of 2002 when I was stationed in Colorado at the Air Force Academy. This was our first time being stationed in the Midwest and there were a lot of sights we had never seen, so we planned a road trip. The grandparents and two cousins visiting from England decided to join us on this sightseeing trip. We rented a large SUV to hold all of us and set off to explore sites in Colorado, Utah, Arizona, and Nevada. One of the highlights of the trip was a stop in Flagstaff, Arizona, to visit the Grand Canyon and do a little hiking around the canyon rim. We decided to spend an entire day at the Grand Canyon, and since we still had two children in strollers, we were a bit limited on where we could go. My two cousins and I really wanted to hike a small portion of the Grand Canyon rim that was not stroller friendly, so we all agreed to split up and meet later that afternoon. We set off to hike along a trail that was just slightly below the rim and along the edge of the canyon. The trail we hiked offered extraordinary uninterrupted views across the canyon that were simply stunning. We hiked about one mile of the trail, stopping frequently for photos pretending to be National Geographic explorers. The day was perfect, without a single cloud in the sky and no rain in the forecast. The Grand Canyon on a sunny day with crystal clear blue skies is one of the most amazing sights in the world.

Towards the end of our hike, we stopped at a rest spot that jutted out into the canyon atop a large granite cliff with handrails for safety. We stopped and took photos and drank some water. Then we noticed it was about time to meet up with the rest of the group. My cousins were behind me as I took one more long view of the canyon, and then all of a sudden and literally out of the blue there was a loud EXPLOSION just to the right of me. Without warning, and with blue skies above us, a lightning bolt struck the ground just to my right and below the canyon with a huge crash. As fate would have it, I was holding the handrails at the time and this blinding flash of light, not more than fifteen yards to my right, also struck me in the top of the head. I did not get hit by the main shaft of the lightning bolt, but instead by a stringer from the main bolt, and it went straight through my body and exited out my left side into the steel railing.

I was shocked, both figuratively and literally, since there was no forecast of thunderstorms that day and there was not a cloud in the sky. There had been absolutely no warning whatsoever. No distant rumbling, no gust front, no raindrops or anything else to warn us that a storm had been forming about ten miles away, just below the rim where we could not see it. This was the first indication the storm was nearby, and the first flash of lightning had to hit me! My cousin exclaimed, "Holy crap, are you OK Jim?"

My cousins had seen the whole thing and could not believe their eyes. Slowly, I emerged from the shock and haze of the strike and replied, "I think I am OK?"

I was not certain if I was OK, but at least I was still standing! I figured the electricity must have flowed through me so quickly that it did not have time to do much damage, but it really hurt like hell and I was in pain. My cousins assessed me, and since we were out on a trail, we really had no choice but to hike to the nearest road and try to get a ride back to the main lodge.

"Wow," my cousin said. "The top of your head is very hot and your hair is a bit singed. You are fortunate to still be here!"

Just my luck, I had been hit by lightning again and in a very unusual manner!

We hiked to the road and flagged down a tour bus that kindly gave us a ride back to the main lodge. As we were boarding the bus, the thunderstorm unloaded all of its fury on the canyon, and what was a calm and very dry day suddenly turned into a torrential downpour with flooding and lightning all around. One of the passengers remarked, "Good thing we came along when we did. Lightning can be very dangerous."

I wanted to say "no shit" but refrained and said, "Yes, I know, I was just struck by lightning, but thank you for the warning!"

I was asked several times how I felt and I kept lying and saying that I was OK. We were on vacation and I did not want an ambulance to take me to the emergency room where I would waste several hours, only to have them tell me everything was fine. My heart was beating, and despite a sore spot on the top of my head and numbness all down my left side and no feeling in my left arm or leg, I was fine. In retrospect, I probably should have gone to the hospital, but being a veteran of one lightning strike, I thought I knew best. The numbness persisted all down my left side for about three days with some pain and discomfort, but I was determined not to let this interfere with our trip. I probably should have been looked at, but everything else seemed OK and after about three days I could feel my left side again, so all was fine.

So what are the odds that someone will be hit by lightning? In my case, they were 100 percent, and to be hit twice nine years apart in such an unusual fashion was clearly a message! I must not have learned my lesson after the first strike, and after surviving another one, I decided it was probably time to take inventory and count all the blessings in my life. I retired from the Air Force after twenty years, so I could pursue other passions, even though I was selected for further promotion. I could have stayed in the Air Force for another seven years, but I decided it was time to focus on my family and other interests. I would go on after the Air Force to lead several non-profit organizations and continue serving others. With a lot of luck, hard work, and good fortune (stopping frequently to enjoy the view along the way), I was able to retire at fifty years old and have never looked back. I just wish it did not take two lightning strikes for me to learn my lesson!

Some People Are Stupid, but Not YOU, Because:

You understand how lucky you are to have this wonderful life and do not need to be struck by lightning twice to realize it!

Chapter 14
It Cannot Be Done

I have been fortunate during my life to find myself often coming up against situations where something new had to be tried or the solution was nearly impossible according to "The Experts." There are various examples I could use, but in every instance, there was someone or something that kept getting in the way of accomplishing the goal and I was repeatedly told, "There is no way to get it done."

I have always been extra motivated by the words of the naysayers: "That has never been done," or, "That's impossible and it will never work."

I love those phrases and, in every case, when I was working on a project, running an organization, or solving a negotiating issue, those words inspired me to think outside the box and find creative and legal ways to get things done. I admit that on a few occasions I did not pull off the impossible, but came close enough that what we did achieve was much more significant than if I had listened to the naysayers. In my world, the best leaders are the ones that question conventional wisdom, listen to their team of experts, and are not afraid to take calculated risks in order to achieve individual and organizational greatness.

In 1997, I was selected to serve as the Military Advisor to the US ambassador to the United Nations in New York City. During this time, the US ambassador to the UN was a senior member of the President's Cabinet and I found myself practicing multi-lateral diplomacy at the highest levels of the US government. My portfolio consisted of all of Africa and Asia, and needless to say, I was very busy crafting the best military and security advice relating to many issues in both of those regions. The days were very long (twelve to fourteen hours) and we worked an average of seventy to eighty hours a week during normal operations, and much more when there was an international crisis. I did not work alone and had many colleagues and peers in State Department, Office of the Secretary of Defense, Joint Chiefs of Staff, The White House, and the National Security Council. In New York, there were several State Department foreign service officers (FSOs) assigned to handle specific countries within Asia and Africa, and in every case, we formed a Political-Military Affairs Policy Team to develop the best advice possible for our ambassador, the US Interagency, and ultimately US Foreign Policy.

There were several FSOs, but only one of me handling quite a large area of responsibility. I focused primarily on issues of the highest US National Security Interest, which were primarily issues brought before the UN Security Council. Most people do not realize that the UN Security Council is in session 365 days a year to handle any evolving or emerging security issues, unlike other UN bodies. We stayed very busy. And particularly when you had Africa, you almost always had an issue before the Security Council. Of all the issues that came before the UN Security Council during my three years in New York, about 70 percent were Africa related. If you talked about disarmament, illegal weapons smuggling/sales, conflict diamonds, children soldiers, women's rights, HIV/AIDS, or addressing an interstate or intrastate conflict, you were likely talking about some region or country in Africa.

One of the ongoing conflicts I had been handling since arriving in New York was the insurgency in the West African country of Sierra Leone. This particular insurgency was very violent, and the rebels known as the Revolutionary United Front (RUF) were fighting the government of Sierra Leone for control of the country, mainly the diamond producing areas. The RUF had been pursuing a campaign of terror and many innocent civilians had been killed, tortured, and taken as prisoners by the RUF and forced to fight or be killed. The United States was working hard to support the government of Sierra Leone and their efforts to end the insurgency, but the government was weak and their military was poorly trained and equipped. The regional alliance known as the Economic Community of West African States (ECOWAS) agreed to form a regional military unit to support the government of Sierra Leone know as the Economic Community Military Observers Group (ECOMOG). The main component of ECOMOG were Nigerian Army Battalions principally assigned to protect the capital of Freetown and occasionally to launch offensive operations against the RUF outside of the capital in the diamond areas. The RUF continued to hold the diamond regions. Conflict diamonds were finding their way of out Sierra Leone and the rebels were able to continue financing their insurgency. The Nigerian battalions were well trained soldiers and very brave, but they were not very well equipped and their logistics supply line was very poor. In other words, the Nigerian Army Units could not bring the fight to the RUF because they could not sustain combat operations once they got a short distance from their base in the capital.

As the military advisor for Africa, I was always trying to find ways to support the government of Sierra Leone and the Nigerian Army battalions so they could do their job. I often ran into roadblocks, and along the way there were several large RUF offensives against the capital of Freetown where thousands of innocent civilians were killed and many Nigerian soldiers lost their lives. I worked closely with my State Department and Pentagon colleagues and found various ways within the framework of United States Code to provide some assistance to the Nigerians; however, it was never enough and much more needed to be done. In the meantime, I was working hard in New York and the US Interagency to help the United Nations put together a peacekeeping operation. We worked non-stop and eventually crafted a UN Security Council Resolution authorizing up to thirteen thousand peacekeeping troops for Sierra Leone. The largest military component of the UN peacekeeping operation would be the Nigerian battalions and we were hopeful that the UN operations would ramp up to speed quickly so that the supply and logistics issues could be resolved.

In March of 2000, I was dispatched by Ambassador Richard Holbrooke to Sierra Leone to visit the Nigerian battalions firsthand and determine exactly what their needs were. I encountered Nigerian battalions that had begun to show some battle fatigue after having successfully defended and recaptured the capital from the rebels about a year earlier and were still defending against sporadic attacks. The Nigerian soldiers were doing the best they could, but clearly they needed a lot more equipment and logistics support to keep going. The United Nations deployment was not going to happen anytime soon since the UN must rely on member states to donate or provide services on a reimbursable basis when it forms a peacekeeping operation, which takes several months. I needed to get something in place as soon as possible to assist the Nigerian battalions before something happened to upset the tentative peace process.

I arrived back in New York and crafted a Sierra Leone trip report that was well received by Ambassador Holbrooke and the entire US Interagency.

"Jim," Ambassador Holbrooke said, "this report contains some key recommendations that I think we need to get behind and push for approval through the US Interagency process."

Ambassador Holbrooke continued, "I will call the President and make the case for these recommendations and help grease the skids for Interagency approval."

"Thank you, Mr. Ambassador," I said, "those recommendations

are based on what I saw and heard from the Nigerian battalions on the front lines."

The report contained concrete observations and recommendations on the way forward in Sierra Leone, and many of those recommendations would eventually be adopted as US foreign policy next steps in Sierra Leone. Chief among these recommendations was getting much needed non-lethal maintenance and logistical support to the Nigerian battalions in Sierra Leone, which were the backbone of the current operation. I worked closely with my peers and colleagues to find a way to provide this support, and every time I came up with another idea, I ran into a roadblock. I had lawyers from the Pentagon and State Department telling me that it was not possible, and although they did not question the need for the support, they simply could not figure out a way of getting it done. I was not deterred and keep working the issue with the approval of my immediate commander and the US ambassador. I was bound and determined to find a way to assist the Nigerian battalions. To complicate matters, the Nigerian battalions were now part of the newly formed United Nations peacekeeping operation just authorized by the UN Security Council. This meant that the Nigerians were "blue helmeted," and as such, the United States was prohibited from providing support directly to the Nigerian battalions as we had been doing prior to the UN peacekeeping operation being approved.

Part of the solution came up in a conversation with a few folks at the National Security Council when I discovered that Section 607 of the Foreign Assistance Act of 1961 might be the answer. The Foreign Assistance Act authorizes the *"President of the United States to furnish goods and services on an advance-of-funds reimbursable basis to friendly countries, international organizations, the American Red Cross, and voluntary non-profit relief agencies registered and approved by the U.S. Agency for International Development (USAID), when the President determines it is in the furtherance of the goals of the Act."*

I discovered under Section 607 that there also needed to be a letter of assist in place with an organization or country detailing the particulars of the service and goods to be provided. After some research, I learned that the United Nations was a registered and approved agency under the Foreign Assistance Act of 1961. The US had simply not concluded a "letter of assist" under the Foreign Assistance Act, or what is called a "607 Agreement," in several years. I found an angle and knew that all we needed to do was sign an updated "607 Agreement" with the UN that detailed the specifics of the support and the final disposition of the support and non-lethal equipment provided. I felt good about this development and had the full support of Ambassador Holbrooke and the White House. I worked tirelessly with the U.S. Interagency approval process and, despite several roadblocks along the way, I managed to conclude a signed letter of assist from the White House. The letter of assist would allow the US to provide $20 million worth of critical, non-lethal equipment and maintenance support to the Nigerian battalions operating within the United Nations peacekeeping operation on a non-reimbursable basis. My colleagues and I were excited, and we had done it in record time!

I thought we were home free. Then I hit what was the biggest roadblock and heard those famous words: "Jim, great effort trying to make this happen, but we cannot conclude the 607 agreement, it is simply not going to be possible," I was told by the Deputy Secretary of Defense.

"What?" I said. "We have a signed letter of assistance and approval from all the relevant agencies?"

"I know," said the Deputy Secretary of Defense. "However, we all overlooked a new piece of legislation that has just been passed by the Senate called the Helms-Biden Act."

The Deputy Secretary continued, "This new legislation now prohibits the United States from providing assistance to a United Nations peacekeeping operation on anything other than a reimbursable basis."

"Oh no," I said. "This new legislation will stop us in our tracks."

I knew the UN would not want to reimburse the US at our rates since they are obligated to use the lowest bidder, which is often not the US. In this case, we were trying to provide this support "in-kind" by providing equipment and logistical support, not actual dollars, and seeking reimbursement at US rates would certainly be a showstopper. This development appeared to stop me dead in the water.

I remained determined to assist the Nigerians battalions serving in the UN peacekeeping operation in Sierra Leone and in May 2000 I got a break. After my trip to Sierra Leone in March 2000, I had indicated that the Nigerian battalions needed logistical support in order to continue protecting the capital of Freetown and support the tentative peace process. As fate would have it, and as feared, the RUF rebels broke the peace agreement. The May Crisis began in the town of Makeni at a Disarmament, Demobilization, and Reintegration site when ten RUF rebels voluntarily disarmed against RUF orders. The RUF demanded the return of their personnel, but the UN did not have them. The rebels had come into the camp, disarmed, collected a stipend from the UN, and then disappeared into the countryside of Sierra Leone. The RUF leaders did not believe or trust the UN, so the situation escalated with an exchange of fire, taking 427 Zambian peacekeepers hostage, and surrounding and laying seize to the encampment of 224 Indian peacekeepers. The situation was critical and in response, the UN accelerated deployment timelines to help stabilize the situation. The UN sent out many requests for all types of airlift, sealift, medical supplies, battalion supplies, etc., but the international community was slow to respond. In the meantime, ten UN peacekeepers were killed and the Indians remained surrounded by the rebels in a very tense situation with almost daily exchanges of fire. The increased visibility of this crisis situation in Sierra Leone brought me much needed publicity and the call for the US to do something to assist. This was the break I needed to get the much-needed logistical support to the Nigerian battalions.

The May Crisis lasted into July as the international community tried to put together a response. The US was still prohibited from support on "other than a reimbursable basis," according to Helms-Biden Legislation, so we were still up against a roadblock. One day in a secure video teleconference meeting with the State Department, White House, DOD, Joint Staff, and the National Security Council, I simply asked, "Given the nature of the current security situation is it possible for the President to sign a waiver allowing the $20 million in logistical support to flow to the Nigerian battalions through the United Nations peacekeeping operation?"

There was silence and I could hear the lawyers thinking about whether the President, acting under the Foreign Assistance Act and determining there was a threat to the internal security of Sierra Leone, and acting in accordance with US foreign policy, could issue a one-time waiver. I will admit that I asked this question more as I was "thinking out loud" and a bit frustrated that we could not get much needed support to Sierra Leone, but I understood the legal challenges. Instead of laughter from the US Interagency, I heard the State Department representative say, "Well, maybe that could happen, let's take a closer look."

I was shocked that we had not thought of this sooner, and a bit surprised I was not laughed out of the meeting. After a few long days and much discussion, giving credit to many great folks involved, we ended up getting a waiver signed by the President that allowed the much needed non-lethal and maintenance support to flow through the UN peacekeeping mission to the Nigerian battalions.

The Sierra Leone Crisis of May 2000 ended in July and the UN continued their deployment to help stabilize the country and keep the peace process on track. The Nigerians were much better supported to assist in any future disruptions to the peace process and this contributed greatly to an eventual, lasting peace in Sierra Leone. Because of the May Crisis and the need for properly trained and equipped peacekeepers in

West Africa, the President would announce a $60 million program called Operation Focus Relief to train and equip seven West African battalions. During a state visit to Nigeria, the President made the announcement that five of the seven battalions receiving the training and assistance would be from Nigeria. The Sierra Leone Crisis had highlighted the Nigerians and the need for well trained and equipped battalions. I know that the actions of myself and several others made this possible in the face of the naysayers that said it could not be done.

Some People Are Stupid, but Not YOU, Because:

You know that when someone says "It cannot be done," or "That's not possible," you are motivated to redouble your efforts and accomplish the nearly impossible or undoable.

Chapter 15
Righteous Indignation

During the spring of 1999, I was travelling through Africa on behalf of the United States ambassador to the United Nations. I was representing the US in peace talks regarding the conflict in the Democratic Republic of the Congo (DRC) and Sierra Leone. The trip had started out in Lusaka, the capital of Zambia, where all of the factions involved in the DRC Conflict had gathered for a peace conference. The conference went well, and along with the US country team from the embassy, I felt good about the talks and the way forward for the DRC. It was one of the first times that all the factions had gathered in one place to discuss a possible settlement in the DRC. I left Lusaka feeling very good about the Comprehensive Peace Plan we negotiated and felt the trip was a huge success, since we had achieved all of our objectives.

As I was leaving Lusaka, I was diverted by my boss to drop into Sierra Leone on my way back and see firsthand how the rebel insurgency there between the government and Revolutionary United Front (RUF) was progressing. The ambassador wanted me to see what assistance we could offer from the United States in order to keep the peace process moving forward. My trip to Sierra Leone, along with assistance from the US ambassador to Sierra Leone and his team, was extraordinary. I gained a much-needed perspective of the actual challenges on the ground, which would eventually drive a US foreign policy I crafted articulating the next steps in Sierra Leone. We had been working hard to end a very brutal insurgency that had cost the lives of thousands of innocent civilians, and this trip helped bring about an end to that conflict. After having travelled from Zambia to South Africa, then onto Angola, Nigeria, Ghana, and Sierra Leone, a long trip through Africa over more than two weeks was finally drawing to an end. I was tired and looking forward to getting home and providing my recommendations for next steps in two conflict zones.

I must admit that part of the adventure of travelling in Africa is the travel itself. Since I was a low ranking military advisor travelling on diplomatic orders, I had to travel via African commercial airlines. This is a challenge in itself, and I quickly learned that flight schedules and departure times were merely suggestive. Most Africans have come to understand that waiting is simply a part of travelling in Africa, and they have mastered the art of waiting patiently for hours on end with little expectation that they will arrive anywhere as planned or scheduled. I had become accustomed to this culture and learned to wait patiently and quietly since I was obviously an American, and with the added scrutiny of travelling on diplomatic orders, I never wanted to create a scene. I was vigilant not to create any disturbances that might possibly reflect badly or somehow cause embarrassment to the United States. Along these lines, I was also very familiar with another African tradition: graft, or corruption.

In preparation for my sub-Saharan travels, I would always take along a large number of US dollar bills to pay for the unexpected, yet fully anticipated, additional charges and fees for a number of things that really had no fee but were imposed as an obvious American diplomat approached. I learned early on that paying a dollar or two here and there, and occasionally more, was easier than creating a scene. Please understand that I am not judging African culture and the unfortunate amount of graft and corruption in sub-Saharan Africa. The vast majority of sub-Saharan Africans live in such extreme poverty that a dollar or two here and there can really make the difference in their daily struggle to survive. If I were in their shoes, I might also take a dollar or two from an

American military diplomat!

I had completed my work in Freetown, the capital of Sierra Leone, and was booked to travel back to the United States through Monrovia, Liberia, then Abidjan, Cote D'Voire, then Paris, and eventually back to New York. My journey was reconfirmed before I left the US embassy, and all my connections and seat assignments were confirmed all the way through. I started my journey at Port Loko, Sierra Leone, on a Russian-built MI-8 helicopter, and then through Liberia on a small regional African airline, and into Abidjan, Cote d'Ivoire, where I would connect to an Air France flight for the journey to Paris. I was pleased to be heading home and the journey to Abidjan was relatively uneventful, other than the usual delays and having to pay a few dollars here and there to get through the security checkpoints, etc.

When I arrived in Abidjan, I had to collect my luggage and then go through another security checkpoint for my follow-on flight to Paris. When I arrived at the security checkpoint, the guards immediately called me out of line and insisted on inspecting all of my luggage, and me, by hand. They were obviously looking for anything of value, particularly US dollars, and they found the very last $20 that I had to my name and decided that I was not allowed to leave their country with any money. They insisted that I could not take money out of their country since I was headed to Paris. However, strangely enough, they did not take any of the African coins and currency I had accumulated during my trip, only the US dollars. I was not upset by any of this, and was quite happy that I had cleared what I thought would be the last hurdle and was now headed out of Africa. Ticket in hand and the Air France flight scheduled to depart on time, I settled into the passenger waiting area to relax until boarding time.

I was pleased the journey had gone so well and I was sitting beside a very pleasant African gentleman from Ghana awaiting the same flight. As we chatted about nothing very much, I felt a hand on my shoulder and a woman's voice asking, "Are you Mr. James Faber?"

"Yes, I am," I said, and turned to see it was a young woman who obviously worked for the airline.

She said, "Sir, I need to talk to you about your seat. Could you please come over to the ticket desk?"

"Of course," I replied, and we walked together to the desk where I thought we might be confirming my final destination or validating my checked luggage.

The woman very politely said, "I am sorry to say that you owe an additional $50 to hold your seat and be allowed to depart Cote d'Ivoire."

I was shocked to say the least, and the grip of African graft had not released its hold just yet. I protested the fee and mentioned that the ticket had been fully paid weeks ago through the US government. However, she was not willing to relent. I told her that all of my US dollars were gone and that I only had a credit card and some African currency left to cover the fee. Of course, she needed the fee in cash due to some airline or airport regulations, which she was obviously making up, but had rehearsed many times in the past. Not wanting to make a scene, I was trying my very best to remain calm and talk her out of this intractable insistence for a bogus fee. She kindly agreed to accept the fee in local currency and pointed out an ATM that conveniently was also located in the waiting area. I was worried that my credit card might not work at an ATM in Western Africa, and of course, it did not. I was now out of ideas, money, and stranded in the Abidjan airport.

I managed to find enough African currency to insert into a nearby payphone to reach an operator that connected me to my contact at the US embassy in Sierra Leone where I had started my journey much earlier in the day. My contact, a state department foreign service officer, stated very plainly that there was little they could do, and by the time something was figured out, I would have missed the flight and faced the prospect of an overnight stay in Abidjan. This was not the option I wanted, since at this point in time I had no contacts in this city and the thought of being stranded in a strange African city is not a very good thing for an American travelling alone. It was at this point that my state department contact simply stated, "You know, Jim, sometimes when I travel through Africa, I find that a bit of Righteous Indignation tends to go a long way."

I had spent the entire trip trying not to cause a scene and now I was being told that I should "raise a little stink" and perhaps the woman would back down. I told him I would give it a try, but to stand by the phone in case there was no movement and I was facing the prospect of an overnight in Abidjan.

I approached the airline desk and the woman who was demanding the $50 fee, and very politely told her that I did not have the money, or any way of paying her. She restated her position that the fee was required or I would not be allowed to board. I began to raise my voice and said, "This is absurd, and your fee is nothing more than embezzlement!"

Several passengers in the waiting area near the desk heard me and began to take notice of what was occurring. "Lower your voice," the woman said. "I cannot do anything about the fee and getting upset will not help the situation."

I raised my voice a bit louder so everyone could hear me. "I insist that you stop asking for a bogus fee that I am certain no other passenger in this waiting area has been asked to pay!"

At this point, more people began to turn and take notice and I could tell the woman was beginning to get a bit nervous. I then insisted on speaking to a supervisor, to which she curtly responded, "There are no supervisors on duty at the moment."

I was determined not to back down and continued to raise my voice until I noticed an African gentleman had appeared just above the waiting area on a sort of balcony space, apparently having emerged from some office.

"Are you in charge?" I asked the man who had appeared on the balcony.

"Yes," he replied and asked, "Please sir, lower your voice."

I explained the situation and that I could not, and at this point would not, pay the extra fee. "Well," the gentleman said, "the fee is required of all departing passengers that are not Cote d'Ivoire citizens as a departure tax."

At this point, I was dumbfounded and stated that I had never heard of something so ridiculous. My anger was very visible and I was getting louder as they continued to insist that I pay the fee. I was not backing down and I replayed my phone conversation with my state department contact. Was I showing too much "righteous indignation"? Had I gone too far? Would they have me arrested by one of their "co-conspirators" since I was on their turf and they were both in on the scam?

Suddenly, a few passengers who were in the waiting area approached the desk and plainly stated that they were not citizens of Cote D'Ivoire. They explained that much like the American they were connecting through Abidjan but had not been charged a "departure tax." This was the turning point, and the woman and gentleman immediately began to back down since it was apparent that they were becoming very anxious by the whole situation. Their little scam had failed and they had no choice but to "waive" the departure tax for me and then politely asked me to calm down. I had no idea this approach was going to work and was afraid I might end up being arrested, but at the end of the day, they were extremely embarrassed when called out by their fellow Africans. At this point, the woman and gentleman wanted nothing more than for me to sit down and be quiet. I obliged promptly and boarded my flight to Paris, which was right on schedule, yet another first during my African adventure!

<u>Some People Are Stupid, but Not YOU, Because:</u>

You realize that there are very few times in our lives where displaying "righteous indignation" is appropriate and understand that only in very rare circumstances when we are absolutely in the right should we take such a forceful stand.

Chapter 16
Decline with Prejudice

I retired from the United States Air Force in 2005 as a lieutenant colonel because I knew it was time for me to move on to other things. A wise commanding officer said to me that "sooner or later we all must leave the Air Force and only you will know when the time is right."

A lot of my Air Force peers have served long and very successful careers and eventually retired when they have reached the maximum time and rank that they can achieve. In my case, I left on my own terms after a little more than twenty years. I was very fortunate to have been "identified" for further promotion to full colonel and could have stayed on active duty for at least another seven to eight years. When I tell other military folks this fact, they do not say much and I always suspect they think, "Yeah, right, you left because further promotion was not going to happen and you wanted to get out before being passed over."

This is not true and in the Air Force, when you promote to lieutenant colonel, the top 10 percent receive an "asterisk" next to their name, which indicates they are senior service school pre-selected candidates. The "asterisk" means that you WILL attend senior service school in residence and the promotion to full colonel after going in residence is 100 percent. In fact, all Air Force officers identified with the "asterisk" are promoted to full colonel at about a 99 percent rate. The reason it is not 100 percent is due to people like me who essentially turn down further promotion by declining to accept the senior service school appointment.

I made the decision to retire simply because my family situation had changed and I did not want to give at least another eight years to the Air Force, totaling about twenty-eight years of service. The Air Force had other ideas and I was selected as an alternate to attend the National War College in my first year of eligibility, which was shortly after I pinned on lieutenant colonel. Alternates typically do not get selected to attend in their first year of eligibility, but again, the Air Force had other plans, and I was selected to attend National War College. Being selected in my first year of eligibility to attend the National War College was truly an honor, but it would force me to make a decision before I was ready. I was hoping to have at least one more year at my current duty station and applied for a deferment through my chain of command. Unfortunately, deferments are only granted for officers that are currently serving in "critical billets" and cannot be moved before the end of their three-year tour. I was not currently serving in a critical billet, and moving me before the end of my three-year tour was well within Air Force regulations.

I studied my options very carefully and considered what would be best for my family, and specifically, my disabled son. My son had been born less than two years earlier with a permanent disability and the timing to move him could not have been worse. We had my son well established with some of the best specialists and therapists in the country and we did not want to move him for at least one more year. Fortunately, the Department of Defense has a program called the exceptional family member program (EFMP). The EFMP program is designed for military families with members who have special needs, so this can be considered when the respective service is looking at reassigning an active-duty member. However, the needs of the service always come first, and although assignment folks take into consideration a member's EFMP status, it is no guarantee you will not be moved. I applied for a one-year waiver under the EFMP program for humanitarian reasons as the regulations allow. However, the waiver was not approved.

After much mental anguish and talking with my wife, who by the way was very supportive either way, I decided it was best to simply retire after twenty years and decline the school appointment and essentially decline promotion to full colonel. This was a very difficult decision for me. I had really loved every day of serving in the Air Force and wished I had not been put in this position at this point in my life/career. Had I not been selected for in-residence school during my first year of eligibility, I would have had at least another year at my current duty station, which had been the original plan. Despite my requests and pleas to delay the school slot for another year, I was given an ultimatum to either take the slot or drop retirement papers. I dropped my retirement papers and left the Air Force after a very successful career in the fall of 2005. I have no regrets or reservations about my decision to retire early and have never looked back.

I am not bitter or angry with the Air Force or their policies regarding school slots and promotions, since this is simply the way it is. I saluted smartly and carried on and I really mean that sincerely. I had a great career, and the Air Force was always good to my family and me. I had several really wonderful assignments and got to do things that most people can only dream about, so I had no regrets. The issue for me in all of this was the paperwork I was required to complete, and more specifically, the language required on one of the forms.

Let me be clear, paperwork is a part of military life, and that caused me zero concern. I even did not mind the language stating that I had turned down the school slot and hence, further promotion. It was bad enough to have made the decision in the first place, but as I completed the paperwork, there was a statement that said I had "Declined with Prejudice" the school slot. What a horrible phrase, and it comes from Air Force Instruction 36-2301 dated 16 July 2010, pages 14-17 and page 19. I could not believe that in order for me to decline this selection, which was already very difficult, I had to decline it with prejudice!

"Are you kidding me?" I said, and requested that the phrase be removed.

It was already hard enough to turn down further promotion, but I was shown the reference and told that nothing could be done to remove the phrase once my humanitarian waiver request had been declined. I do not know if that AF instruction or that phrase is still being used today, but in 2005 it was, and I had to acknowledge and sign that I was declining with prejudice.

What does declining with prejudice even mean? Does it mean that I am REALLY, REALLY declining and that there is absolutely no turning back? It seemed to me that this was pouring salt into the wound and served no useful purpose. Whoever penned that phrase and worked it into an Air Force regulation should be held accountable with prejudice for being so mean. It is not like I did not serve honorably over the past twenty-plus years. In fact, the Air Force was so pleased with my performance that they had essentially selected me for further promotion. This language was like the snapping of a bone, and perhaps whomever thought of it was hoping that folks would find it so offensive that they would change their mind. Who knows? In any case, I "declined with prejudice" and was honorably retired from the Air Force and even given a Meritorious Service Medal for my twenty-plus years of service— perhaps I should have declined the medal with prejudice!! Just kidding!!

Some People Are Stupid, but Not YOU, Because:

You understand that you do not need to rub salt into someone's wound. It will only cause more harm and serve no useful purpose.

Chapter 17
Greatness

I am on a mission to preserve the word "Hero" for those that are truly great. I sometimes hear people talk about their heroes and why they hold them in such high regard. For many folks, heroes are exceptional human beings that have done something extraordinary, leaving an indelible impression. Everyone has a hero, but the definition of hero is certainly not consistent from one person to the next. I am not questioning whether someone's hero is legitimate or not, but what I will say is there are certainly different "levels" of heroes, and when we look beyond our own definition of the word, we begin to see that not all heroes are created equally. In some cases, I have heard the word "hero" overused and misapplied to really good people, but not necessarily people who have done something heroic. To me, heroes are Great Human Beings that have done something extraordinary while putting the wellbeing of others ahead of their own. When I am in the presence of a true hero, they inherently exude a sense of humbleness, commitment, selflessness, and greatness.

During my career, I have been very fortunate to be in the presence of extraordinary people that have accomplished so much in their lives. All of them were impressive in their own right and had truly made selfless choices to serve others, but that did not necessarily make them all great. I have had the privilege of being around senior military officers and commanders, heads of state from many countries, senior US Administration officials, sports figures, actors, wealthy individuals, and the President of the United States. Each of these people served others in their own ways and led lives of service in one way or another.

Just because you have been very successful and achieved the rank of four-star general, or Secretary of Defense or State, or even the President, this in itself does not make you great. These people are driven and very intelligent, despite your politics, they deserve respect for their accomplishments, and in many cases praise for their selfless decisions to be public servants. And trust me, they are very impressive men and women. This caliber of person tends to put the needs of others, their countries, and constituents at the forefront. Of course, there are people in these senior positions that are not selfless and may be corrupt or self-serving, but in this essay, I am focusing on the great number I encountered that were selfless. I am not going to list all of the people I had the wonderful opportunity to meet and work with/for, but trust me, I have had enough exposure to determine what is greatness, at least by my standards.

I was around so many individuals with rank, status, fame, etc., that I was not "star struck," I became used to being around such people and took it for granted after awhile. I do not say this to brag, only to bring perspective that for someone among this group of very distinguished individuals to leave an impact on me and be characterized as truly "Great" and a "Hero" was an accolade I did not easily bestow. As I stated at the beginning of this essay, the definition of the word hero will vary from one person to the next and it is truly an experiential definition. The more people we meet in our lifetimes, the broader our experiences and the greater exposure to truly great men and women.

Heroes in the post-9/11 World

Prior to 9/11, anyone serving in the military did not hear, "Thank you for your service" very often, if at all. I never heard it, and the baby boomer generation really did not like the military very much due to the Vietnam War and the politicization of that conflict. A large percentage of my generation had very poor attitudes and behaviors towards men and women serving in the military. I recall walking around the campus of Boston University in my ROTC uniform being yelled at and heckled by fellow students and passersby. It was not nearly as bad as what others had encountered in the late sixties and seventies, but it was enough of an issue that we only wore our uniforms when we had an official ROTC event (leadership class, drill, parades, etc.). I am thrilled that the United States has finally gotten over this sad time in our history, and I am proud when people say thank you for your service and I have learned to simply say thank you.

The post-9/11 world is much better for folks serving in the military, veterans, and retirees. All of the men and women that serve have truly made a choice to put others before themselves and serve this great country. This is to be commended, applauded, and thanked, but not everyone that wears a uniform is a hero simply because they put it on. In the years following 9/11, I have travelled quite a bit, and now I see military members travelling in their uniforms when in my day it was prohibited, or certainly frowned upon, due to the possible conflict it may cause. Today, young men and women want to travel in their uniforms and are treated with respect and dignity, and the public shows great pride; I applaud this with every ounce of my being. However, I am not in agreement that these men and women are all heroes just because they joined the military. I have been waiting in line to board an airline and the boarding agent allows service members in uniform to board first and they are often upgraded to better seats and I say "bravo." What bothers me is that often the agent will state that these men and women are our heroes. I agree we should treat them with dignity and respect, but heroes, I do not know.

Certainly these men and women are selfless and deserve the upgrade perks, respect, etc., of all fellow Americans, but until I am aware that they have done something "great" where they put others ahead of themselves, I think the word hero should be reserved. We need to stop overusing this word and apply it to cases where people are truly heroes (Medal of Honor recipients, rushing into a burning building to rescue others, charging hijackers on a plane, combat medals for heroism, taking a political stand or human rights stance that lands you in prison, etc.). I am sorry, but this is just one example of the overuse of the word hero in the public mind and I do not believe that simply enlisting in the military or becoming a first responder automatically makes you great or a hero. Of course, these career fields, and many others, are the first step in becoming truly great, since they may provide the opportunity for heroic actions, which could lead to greatness.

Not all people who are in positions of great trial, or find themselves in these circumstances, will act heroically, but the ones that do are truly great. We have many examples of heroic men and women throughout history that were, and are, truly great human beings. In the summer of 2000, I was working as the Military Advisor for Africa to Ambassador Richard Holbrooke and he wanted to host an Africa Summit at the United Nations in New York to discuss the many issues and challenges facing Africa. Ambassador Holbrooke knew that the majority of issues before the UN Security Council were Africa related, and for those of us that worked US–African Policy, this was very exciting. The plan was to have a summit discussing everything from good governance to conflict resolution, arms smuggling, conflict diamonds, child soldiers, HIV/AIDS, humanitarian aid, refugees, and internally displaced persons. The summit would bring together many of the world's leaders to include significant elder statesmen from the African continent to start an ongoing dialogue about these critical issues. Leaders from every African state travelled to New York from the continent, along with the leaders of many of the world's great powers, particularly those that had interests in Africa. Celebrities with African interests also attended the summit, to include Bono from U2 who has worked tirelessly for African debt relief and Whoopi Goldberg who had a strong interest in Africa and human rights issues, among others.

Ambassador Holbrooke also invited Nelson Mandela to attend the summit, but it was not certain if he could make it and we worked very hard to bring all the logistics together so that he could attend. Having one of the greatest African leaders attend the summit would lend it a great deal of transparency and credibility, so we worked very hard to make it happen. Only a few days before the summit, we received confirmation that Nelson Mandela would attend the African Summit. I had never met Mr. Mandela and only knew him from his public life as an anti-apartheid revolutionary, politician, and philanthropist. I was well aware of Mr. Mandela's efforts to end apartheid and his nearly thirty years imprisoned in South Africa for his political views. I had no idea what it would be like to meet him, and as I have mentioned earlier, I had been around a lot of impressive people and this would be just another one.

The day Mr. Mandela arrived, Ambassador Holbrooke was his personal escort while I was busy running around handling details of the summit and dealing with a large number of government officials and VIPs. I was in the Security Council's private chambers and discussions about African issues were about to get started. I was waiting for Ambassador Holbrooke to arrive and I was not certain if Mr. Mandela was attending this session or not. I looked down the hall and there was Ambassador Holbrooke walking towards me supporting the arm of Nelson Mandela. I recall seeing a very gentle, frail man with a wonderful smile on his face and a presence and warmth that seemed to emanate from him. It was very cold in New York and not being used to it, Mr. Mandela was wearing a large fur hat to keep him warm and I recall thinking, *Is he warm enough?* (In 2000, he was eighty-one years old.)

The greatness of the man and the frailness of his body were a very strange juxtaposition and his humbleness was mind-boggling. Ambassador Holbrooke approached and introduced me, "President Mandela, allow me to present Major Jim Faber who serves as my African Advisor."

"A true honor," I said, "and a great privilege to have you in New York for this very important summit."

President Mandela extended his hand and said, "I am honored to be here and I appreciate all the hard work you have done putting this summit together."

"Thank you," I said, while holding Mandela's hand.

I was immediately overcome with a feeling of the greatness of this man and it resonated throughout my core, a real visceral feeling that I cannot really explain. Mandela was so warm, humble, and unassuming that it caught me off guard. He was a brilliant and lovely man! I felt extraordinarily blessed to meet, in my opinion, one of the greatest moral authorities of the twentieth century. I had only rarely experienced this type of feeling in the presence of other great individuals, and this was clearly a unique moment. President Mandela had spent his whole life serving others, and paid with his own freedom so that other South Africans could live more freely. Nelson Mandela was truly great and remains one of my personal heroes to this day.

Some People Are Stupid, but Not YOU, Because:

You understand that "True Greatness" is much more than simply being famous, rich, a celebrity, music legend, or reality TV star, but rather it is something more visceral that you feel from your core while in the presence of Greatness.

Chapter 18
What Are the Odds?

E very year in the United States, the Centers for Disease Control and Prevention estimates that approximately ninety-six thousand Americans will contract e-coli O157:H7 food poisoning. E-coli is potentially deadly bacteria that tends to target our most vulnerable populations, the young and the old. Many folks that contract e-coli will become very sick for about ten days and make a full recovery without any need for hospitalization or serious threat of death. E-coli is mostly transmitted as a food-borne pathogen and the leading culprit tends to be ground beef, although e-coli can also be transmitted by other foods and different methods, such as person-to-person and animal contact.

The current population of the United States is approximately 322 million. So that means only about .0003 percent of the US population will contract e-coli in any given year, which means most of us will never have any issue, or contact, with this potentially deadly bacteria. Of those US citizens that are unlucky enough to become infected with e-coli, only about 26 percent will require hospitalization. An even a fewer number, about 6 percent, will contract the more serious life-threatening complication of e-coli O157:H7 called hemolytic uremic syndrome (HUS). HUS attacks the body's red blood cells and internal organs, often resulting in acute kidney failure, the destruction of red blood cells, and the general assault on the human body causing the shutdown of various systems. In fact, the toxins created by e-coli (Shiga toxin) are so dangerous that the Department of Homeland Security has classified them as a potential bioterrorist agent.

For my two youngest boys, the odds of contracting e-coli O157:H7 food poisoning ended up being 100 percent in the fall of 2005. We were attending a work picnic, and unknown to all of us, the frozen beef patties that were being prepared would end up being part of a national recall of contaminated ground beef. The folks preparing the patties had been very cautious, and they even threw away the first batch since they felt the BBQ flame was too hot and the patties had not cooked all the way through. The next several batches were well cooked and any e-coli in the patties had been killed, but the e-coli was still alive on the spatula, which the food preparers did not think to clean before reusing. Unfortunately, my boys were among the first to have a freshly well-cooked hamburger containing live e-coli from the contaminated spatula. After the first batch, the e-coli on the spatula had been passed along and the rest of the burgers were cooked sufficiently to kill the e-coli that they were carrying. Thankfully, no one else at the work picnic contracted e-coli, but the burgers they had been serving were confirmed as part of a million-pound recall of hamburgers across the US.

My boys started to feel a bit sick within a few days after the picnic. We had no idea what was going on and thought it was some kind of twenty-four-hour bug that would quickly pass. We were wrong, and the boys were getting sicker by the day and starting to become dehydrated due to constant diarrhea. We took them into the emergency room where the physicians also incorrectly diagnosed them as having some kind of bug that would pass and gave them IV fluids and sent them home. The boys got worse, and they also started to pass blood in their diarrhea, at which point we decided they needed better care and took them to the local children's hospital. Since this is a story about odds, it would be our good fortune that the attending physician at the children's hospital had some experience with e-coli poisoning and had a strong "degree of suspicion" when he assessed the boys.

The attending physician immediately ordered some of the boys' stool to be cultured to confirm his suspicion of e-coli, but this could take thirty-six to forty-eight hours to confirm. In the meantime, my oldest of the two boys had a seizure, and it was the first time that my wife and I realized we were dealing with something much more than a simple stomach bug. The doctor immediately ordered that the boys be transported by ambulance to a more advanced and better-equipped children's hospital. He remained suspicious that this could be e-coli and knew the other hospital would be better equipped to handle this crisis. Of course, the results of the stool culture came back a day later and confirmed that our boys had somehow contracted e-coli O157:H7. This was the beginning of a very long and dark journey.

My wife and I did not know a whole lot about e-coli, other than it was very dangerous and could be life threatening. To make matters worse, the lab also confirmed that the boys not only had contracted e-coli, but the much more severe life-threatening complication of hemolytic uremic syndrome (HUS). The doctors were scrambling to save our boys' lives, and they were both admitted to the intensive care unit where we would all become permanent residents for the next forty-five days. We quickly learned about e-coli and what the possible complications could be. At every turn, the boys just got sicker, and when we thought we had hit the bottom, we continued to fall further. The journey was like diving into a black bottomless pit and hitting the sides once in a while, thinking you have finally hit bottom, but then falling further with no end in sight. We could not see any light.

The boys were sick and very uncomfortable, and despite what the doctors did, the e-coli proved to be a formidable enemy. My youngest of the two did start to make a slight recovery and would eventually leave the hospital about two weeks later. My other son was not so fortunate, and went into complete kidney failure requiring peritoneal dialysis, which proved to be ineffective. The doctors then tried the more traditional hemodialysis to clean his system of the toxins that his kidneys were no longer removing from his bloodstream. The hemodialysis was partly successful, but he was so filled with toxins from his kidney failure and the ongoing battle with the e-coli and HUS that his system could not keep up. My son would go on to have many more seizures, several strokes, and require an airway tube and a breathing machine to keep him alive. Every time we thought we had hit rock bottom, something else would happen, and the little guy barely hung onto life. The crash cart for a cardiac arrest was a permanent fixture in my son's room and there were many times it looked like it was the end. He was connected to every machine possible, with tubes, IVs, and monitors attached to every inch of his small body. To make matters worse, we could not hold him or do anything to comfort him other than grip his tiny hand and continue to talk to him.

My son was on anti-seizure medication, heart medicine, blood pressure medication, and many more too numerous to list. He had total kidney failure, was continuing to have seizures and strokes, had part of his intestines removed after they were killed by the e-coli, and had to undergo several surgeries for other issues. In addition, he was undergoing blood transfusions, platelet transfusions, emergency CT scans, brain scans, and was in a medically induced coma on full life support. Every time the doctors got one body system somewhat under control and stabilized, another system would begin shutting down, and it always felt as though we were behind the curve and not catching a break.

Throughout this terrible ordeal, we refused to face the possibility that we might lose him. In the intensive care unit, there is a woman who makes a bronze cast of a child's foot that unfortunately loses the battle and this becomes a cherished memory for the family. The "bronze boot" lady, as my wife and I came to know her, was "on call" for our son and was checking every day on his status. Much later, we would learn that most of the intensive care staff had quietly thought to themselves that it was just a matter of time before my son lost the battle.

I distinctly recall a conversation during this darkest time with my wife. "Suzanne," I said with hesitation, "we may need to start preparing ourselves for the possibility that our son may never come home."

Suzanne immediately fired back, "No way, I am not going there and he will be coming home to make a full recovery!"

In this moment, I saw the intense love and fury of a mother determined to fight until the very end. I thought how silly of me to even bring this up!

I replied, "You are right, there is no need to go there. We will continue to pray and hope for the best."

This subject never came up again!

In the middle of this, our oldest son also became ill and was admitted to the hospital as well; we now had three children in the hospital, all in different wards, so my wife and I became well known as we travelled around the hospital. It would turn out that my oldest son did not have e-coli, but was showing sympathetic symptoms due to the stress of having his two younger brothers so ill. Having three children in the hospital at one time was a very dark moment. We scanned the blackness all around and in front of us, hoping that there might be a small speck of light in the distance, but we continued to fall into the blackness.

My wife and I never lost hope that we would eventually see light again, and this hope, along with the grace of God, kept us strong for our son. At this point, my son had been in total kidney failure for over thirty days, and the doctors were about to declare him in complete end-stage renal failure. The prospect of hemodialysis the rest of his life was a far better outcome than the unimaginable thought of not bringing him home at all. On the last day of my son's kidney failure, when the doctors were about to declare him in end-stage renal failure, we witnessed a miracle. At the very last possible minute, my son actually produced a few drops of urine. The doctors were excited and did not declare him in end-stage renal failure. And finally, after a month of falling, we began to see a small light at the end of the tunnel.

My son would continue to improve, and the light got brighter, and after seven weeks in the hospital, we finally got to take our son home. His recovery took another six months at home, with many ups and downs. He was readmitted to the hospital for a few issues along the way, but we focused on the glimmer of light and followed it until we were once again in the bright light of the day. Every day we are thankful to God that our son is alive, although a bit worse for wear, but very much alive and thriving!

Some People Are Stupid, but Not YOU, Because:

You understand that no matter how bad or dark things get, there will always be a light at the end of the tunnel, regardless of how long or horrific the journey.

Chapter 19
Leadership Is a Journey, Not a Destination

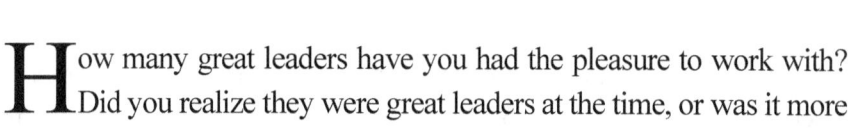

How many great leaders have you had the pleasure to work with? Did you realize they were great leaders at the time, or was it more reflective after the fact? Did they have any sense that they were a great leader? What qualities made them a good leader?

The answers to these questions will vary as many times as they are asked, but one thing is certain, we all need better leadership, and more of it. In the United States alone, approximately $166 billion is spent annually on leadership and training programs! I personally have attended numerous leadership schools, trainings, and seminars, and at one point in my career was a certified leadership instructor. I also have practical leadership experience gained from both my military career and non-profit and for-profit careers. But does that make me a good leader? I have no idea, but at least it provides a basis from which to share my thoughts and opinions on what I think makes a leader effective. There are no right answers on what makes a good leader, but there is some consensus around the key qualities that tend to be present in most successful leaders. I am not going to repeat what has been written in tens of thousands of leadership books, but will share my thoughts on leadership.

Leadership, simply stated, is the ability to persuade people to do something they would not have otherwise done, while convincing them it was their idea all along. There are many theories, volumes of research, and accumulated leadership data that one can study to find the best approach toward motivating people to get the job done, but at the end of the day, it is about relationships and hard work. Nobody will listen to or follow a leader they do not like or do not have any respect for in most cases, with the exception of the military, where disobeying a "lawful order" could result in serious consequences! This is not to say that military leaders are not great leaders. In fact, many military leaders are great leaders and go on to have very successful leadership careers in the civilian sector. What I am trying to say is that just because you were a great leader in the military does not guarantee that you will be a great leader in the civilian sector.

Leadership is not automatically transferable from one leadership environment to another. The best leaders adapt to every leadership challenge and determine the optimal way to move forward. Good leaders are competent, hard-working, evolve and adapt to the current leadership challenge, and build relationships with the team to get the job done. In a good environment, the team will become self-motivated and the leader only has to provide the expectations and then get out of the way while the team accomplishes the task at hand. Great leaders make it look easy and understand that leadership is a bit like electricity, quietly working in the background going unnoticed until the power goes out. The goal of a good leader is to make leadership look easy so others will someday want your job and the chance to lead. Your legacy as a great leader may not be appreciated until someone you have led gets the chance to lead and realizes how much work it takes to sit in the corner office.

How do you know if you are a good leader?? You may never really know since you are not the one to declare that you are a good leader; that assessment lies with the people you have led. If you are lucky, you will get feedback from up and down your chain about your leadership style, how effective, or ineffective, it has been, and ways to improve. We can all be better leaders, regardless of where we are in our lives and careers. The person who claims that he/she is a good leader should be avoided when possible, since they tend to have narcissistic tendencies and usually create toxic environments. The people who state they have taken all the most prestigious leadership trainings and know a thing or two about leadership and have arrived at the "mountaintop of leadership" should also be avoided.

Leadership is an ongoing learning experience, which is why this chapter is titled, Leadership is a Journey, Not a Destination. As we gain more training and experience, I believe we can become better leaders if we are honest and humble about our abilities and shortcomings and endeavor to be lifelong learners. Below is my short list of key leadership qualities that I think makes great leaders. This list is not all-inclusive by a long shot, but I submit that if you try to incorporate these qualities into your approach to leadership, you will be successful.

1. Good Leaders Are Humble and a Bit Vulnerable: Leaders must not assume that they always have the answers or that their way is always the best way. Good leaders listen to their team and synthesize all the inputs to arrive at a way forward to accomplish the task/project at hand. The chosen way forward typically pulls in the best of the team's recommendations, and in-turn, gets buy-in from the team. In many situations, having buy-in is an important component—especially in the civilian leadership world. As a leader, be humble and acknowledge, "I did not think of that approach," to show your team that you are human and that they bring value to the mission, task, project, etc. Finally, good leaders admit when they are wrong or that the selected approach was not the best way forward.

2. Good Leaders Are Confident and Approachable: Confidence in one's ability to make decisions and lead is absolutely a key quality. I am not suggesting that leaders be "cocky," but that they have an "air of confidence" about their approach to decisions and not waiver with the wind and second guess the decisions they have made. This, of course, does not preclude a good leader from making a mid-course correction if required. And this gets to the second point: be approachable. We all know the story about the "King's New Suit" and the inability of those

around him to point out the obvious truth. Leaders make decisions after much thought, deliberation, and debate, and they are confident in the path they have chosen. No leader should be blind after making a decision and should allow team members to provide honest feedback on the path chosen so corrections can be made. Keep communication and feedback channels open and clear from interference!!

3. Good Leaders Have Physical and Emotional Energy: Have you ever worked for or followed a leader and found yourself saying, "How does he/she get everything done?" Leaders have both physical energy to accomplish the daily tasks and also go into hyper-mode when the project or task requires it. This means that leaders tend to keep themselves in good physical shape so they can do what it takes to accomplish a particular task, project, or mission. This is not to suggest that in order to be a good leader you need to be a "workaholic." In fact, just the opposite is true. Everyone works hard and also understands that they must play harder to maintain a healthy work/life balance. Leaders that are workaholics are really not good leaders at all since they have failed to delegate to the team and feel they need to do, or oversee, everything! Most good leaders have a physical, emotional, and intellectual energy that is contagious and inspires the whole team to jump in and get stuff done. I cannot define this energy with much more precision, but I know leaders must lead from the front, and this requires intellectual maturity, emotional stability, and physical ability.

4. Good Leaders Praise Often When the Team Achieves a Goal or Milestone: Do not be stingy with your praise; this is what your followers want most. Praise when the team and/or individuals excel at a task and do it publicly with a bullhorn. Do not "over praise" but adapt to the needs of your team and/or individuals, understanding that some teams require more praise more often and others do not.

5. Good Leaders Are Competent: Know your job and the job you are asking your team to perform. This does not mean you have to be the

SOME PEOPLE ARE STUPID, BUT NOT YOU!

expert on every task performed, but you must have a good working knowledge of what a task requires so that you can set reasonable expectations and provide the required resources.

6. <u>Good Leaders Know Their Team and Show Compassion:</u> Not everyone has a great day every day. Sometimes teams and/or team members have bad days, make mistakes, or are running low on energy for some reason. Never forget you are working with humans and not machines. Show compassion when things fall short and try to help the team get back on track.

7. <u>Good Leaders Delegate and Get Out of the Way:</u> No one likes a micro-manager or a manager that "over manages"! Task your team, provide guidance and support as needed, and get out of the way. Learn to delegate!

8. <u>Good Leaders Create Good Leaders:</u> Challenge your followers and create opportunities where they get to lead according to their ability. You are training your replacement.

9. <u>Good Leaders Are Curious:</u> Do not assume that just because something has always been done a certain way that it is the best way. Challenge yourself and those around you to think in new and innovative ways to develop a better mousetrap. Do not rest on your laurels.

10. <u>Good Leaders Understand That a Brutal Debrief Makes the Team and the Next Project Better:</u> Do not be afraid to speak the truth when you are developing lessons learned and create an environment where people can be honest in their feedback without fear of retribution. Honest and respectful feedback delivered correctly can make the difficult truths more palatable while creating an atmosphere of learning. Always enter a debrief as friends and leave as friends with a plan to apply the lessons learned toward the next project or task.

<u>Some People Are Stupid, but Not YOU, Because:</u>

You understand that leadership is a journey, not a destination, and you also understand that leadership is not universal. Just because you are a good leader in one situation does not automatically guarantee that you will be a good leader in every situation. Good leaders must evolve and adapt their style to the situation.

www.ingramcontent.com/pod-product-compliance
Lightning Source LLC
Chambersburg PA
CBHW060539130626
46553CB00002B/823